TODAY'S GOOD NEWS

General Editor: The Rev. David Field

Consulting Editors: The Rev. John Stott
The Rev. Dr Leighton Ford

Born into Battle

Born into Battle

Paul's two letters to the Thessalonian Christians

EDDIE GIBBS

Illustrated by Annie Vallotton

Collins/Fount Paperbacks

Church Pastoral Aid Society
Falcon Books

First published in Fount Paperbacks 1977

Text © Edmund Gibbs 1977
Illustrations © Collins/Falcon Books
Good News Bible, Today's English Version:
Old Testament © American Bible Society,
New York, 1976

British usage edition reproduced here by kind
permission of the British & Foreign Bible Society

Made and printed in Great Britain by
William Collins & Co Ltd, Glasgow

CONTENTS

1 Thessalonians

Dear Thessalonians

(1:1)

This letter is as genuine as the one on the mantelpiece propped up behind the clock. Because it is part of the Bible we can easily overlook this fact. It isn't in an envelope but bound into a lengthy book, and the form and lay-out do not suggest a letter. There is no sender's address, date, 'Dear . . .' or 'Yours sincerely . . .' In New Testament times the style of letter-writing was different. Letters began with the name of the sender, the people addressed and a formal greeting. And that's how this letter begins.

YOURS SINCERELY

From Paul, Silas and Timothy – Paul writes on behalf of all three, for it was they who formed the team which originally took the gospel to Thessalonica. As a result of their visit, a new church was born. (Read all about it in Acts 17:1-9) Although time and distance now cut off the missionaries from these new Thessalonian believers, they had not shrugged off their concern for them. They prayed for them often, discussed their situation, and they agreed about the message they sent in this letter.

Although Paul was a great individualist, he was no loner. On each missionary journey he took a number of hand-picked travelling companions with him. On his second missionary trip, Silas was his 'number two', a mature and experienced assistant, who was a respected member of the church in Jerusalem. In contrast, Timothy was a raw and

9

timid recruit, enlisted by Paul at Lystra when he was travelling through Galatia. Timothy had been taught the Scriptures from his childhood. This formed the solid basis from which Paul led him to a personal trust in Christ. His life was from that moment under new management.

Now Timothy needed to leave the shelter and security of home to be toughened by combat experience, and to learn by watching men of God as he worked under their direction.

No Christian leader can do it all by himself. Even if he has gifts and experience, he needs a support team to encourage him. It is their job to back him up and build on his teaching. Behind the three men on the Apollo moon flight were thousands of technologists who designed and manufactured the

The gospel was gossiped along.

equipment, programmed the computers, monitored the health of the astronauts, and organized the phase-by-phase sequence of the entire project.

To the people of the church in Thessalonica. All the places Paul addresses in his letters are cities. From the Acts account of his missionary journeys we know that his plan was to follow the Roman trunk-road system to the provincial capitals. These were the great centres of population, political influence, trade and education. It was important to start churches in such places. They could then become launching pads for mission, as the gospel was gossiped along the trunk roads from place to place.

The world of Paul's day was 2.5% urban. Today, it is around 50%. By the turn of the century it is forecast the figure will reach 90% in some regions of the world. Now, more then ever, the spiritual battle is on for the cities.

Paul is writing to a special group of people in Thessalonica. They are *the people of the church*. When Paul writes 'church' he doesn't have in mind a building with tower or spire, pointed windows and a heating problem. By 'church' Paul means people – groups of believers who met in any convenient place. The church had no purpose-built meeting places during its first 300 years.

Why did these Christians arrange to meet together on a regular basis? Because they now *belong to God the Father and the Lord Jesus Christ*. Previously, their lack of faith and selfish ways had cut them off from God. Then Paul preached to them. They heard how God had sent his Son into the world. Jesus came to provide a way by which they could be forgiven and reconciled to God. Then they could be adopted into his family and could call him *Father*. People can only do this when they make *Jesus Christ Lord*, which means supreme controller of life.

Becoming children of God results in believers belonging to one another as members of his family, a miraculously

11

created community which worships God, shares the teaching of Jesus and shows his love and mutual care in action.

ALL THE BEST!

May grace and peace be yours. Christian love transforms polite but empty greetings into sincere, simple prayers. Paul uses two of the most powerful words in the Christian's vocabulary to put his feelings into words. 'Grace' is a word we don't often use today. When 'Amazing Grace, how sweet the sound' hit the pop charts, many people did not know what the word meant – unless it was a girl's name! Paul uses it to describe God's forgiveness. It is quite free and does not depend on our goodness or efforts. Instead it comes to us because Jesus died on the cross. There he took the punishment we should have had for our sins. It means the power he puts within us to live the Christian life. And it includes the many spiritual resources with which he equips us for his service.

'Peace' is the traditional Hebrew greeting. The 'shalom' is exchanged to this day between Jews. Peace does not mean the opportunity to relax and put your feet up, but the strength to keep your head above the waves in a stormy sea. It combines the ideas of inner calm, well-being, harmony and prosperity. It is not a peace which is liable to be shattered at any moment. It is a deep-seated calm which persists in spite of disappointments, dangers or sorrows. 'Peace is what I leave with you; it is my own peace that I give you. I do not give it as the world does. Do not be worried and upset; do not be afraid.' These were Jesus's own words (see John 14:27).

This kind of peace is ours as a result of receiving 'grace'. It is heaven in the heart.

A contagious faith

(1:2-10)

Your local church may have a long history reaching back into the dim, distant past. The one in Thessalonica was only months old – just a toddler, and hardly old enough to be left on its own. But Paul had no choice. Jealous Jews had hired a mugging gang, who attacked the home of his host Jason. When they found that Paul was not there, they dragged Jason and some of the other Christians before the city authorities. The charges brought against Paul and his converts were treason and subversion. 'These men have caused trouble everywhere!' shouted their accusers. 'They

Jealous Jews had hired a mugging gang.

are all breaking the laws of the Emperor, saying that there is another king, by the name of Jesus.' However, as the evidence was scanty and the ringleaders of the new movement were not in court, the authorities demanded that Jason and his friends hand over a substantial cash deposit which they would forfeit if there was any further trouble.

Paul and his team could no longer carry on working in Thessalonica. For the sake of the safety of the Christians who had their homes there, they lost no time in leaving. Travelling on to Berea and Athens, Paul wondered and worried over the fate of the converts he had left behind. In recent times, missionaries forced out of China, Burma, Cambodia and Vietnam have known the same nagging anxiety.

The moment came when Paul could not bear the uncertainty any longer. He sent Timothy back to Thessalonica to find out what was happening. He would be able to encourage the new believers and to report back on how they were getting on.

After an absence which must have seemed like an eternity, Timothy returned with thrilling news. The Christians were not only surviving the hostilities, but thriving in spite of them. So, in relief, joy and gratitude to God, Paul writes, **We always thank God for you all and always mention you in our prayers.** Over and over again he pours out his thanks for their progress, whilst still keeping them on his 'intensive care' list. He prays **always,** not just now and again when he feels in the mood. And he prays for them **all,** not merely for a favourite few. Paul's continuing prayers did for their faith what a thick overcoat would have done for their bodies in a British winter – provided a protective covering!

Especially he rejoices over the quality of their faith.

IT IS A DOWN-TO-EARTH FAITH

What makes a man put his back into a job? Hope of promotion? Desire to protect himself against getting his name on the redundancy list? Satisfaction in doing a job thoroughly?

Christians have a special reason for working hard – to show that their faith makes a practical difference to life between Mondays and Fridays as well as on Sundays.

. . . we remember . . . how you put your FAITH into practice, how your LOVE made you work so hard, and how your HOPE in our Lord Jesus Christ is firm.

'Faith' is no airy-fairy feeling. It is something intensely practical, showing us what needs to be done and assuring us that it can be done. Faith is the driving force which overcomes our reluctance, laziness and that 'Oh, what's the use' kind of feeling. It relates to and transforms the whole of life. The toil is still there, but the sense of drudgery has gone.

Christians don't work with a chip on the shoulder, or with a couldn't-care-less attitude. They work eagerly and wholeheartedly, out of love. By 'love' Paul does not mean 'the milk of human kindness' but a special, supernatural kind of loving. It was first shown to the world on the hill of Calvary, where Jesus died. Christ now makes that love available to his people. As they put their ambitions, thoughts and feelings in his care, so he fills their lives. 'Sweat' is the price tag on this divine love. It does much more than make the heart flutter. It demands initiative, action, sacrifice – in a nutshell, hard labour for life. God's love is meant to fill the Christian's life, flood the church, and fan out through the world.

In the Bible, the word 'hope' does not suggest something beyond our grasp, something that is always round the next bend, but something so certain that it is as good as ours now. It is not like hoping against hope for a pay rise. It is like expecting to find it in next month's pay packet because the increase has already been awarded. Hope is not based on a sentimental faith in people that can be shattered so quickly. It is a natural spin-off from a rock-firm faith in Christ. It looks forward to a great future – a future which Christ has already secured and will ultimately fill. The Christian can therefore keep going in present difficulties with more than a hazy feeling that everything will come out right in the end. Certainty is the note clearly struck by hope in the Bible.

Faith, love and hope are basic ingredients of the Christian life. Faith dispels cynicism; love makes working for God heart-warming; hope banishes gloom. A life filled with these qualities is just as relevant and inspiring now as it was when Paul wrote this letter.

IT IS A SUPERNATURAL FAITH

Our brothers, we know that God loves you and has chosen you to be his own. For we brought the Good News to you, not with words only, but also with power and the Holy Spirit, and with complete conviction of its truth.

A Cummings cartoon in the *Daily Express* shows a bishop in a new 'uniform'. His hat is pulled down over his eyes. On the chain around his neck is not a cross but a question mark. Down one of his gaiters is written 'Thou shalt not necessarily believe in God', and down the other, 'Thou shalt not commit adultery – except in extenuating circumstances'. It's a depressing picture. Do you know a person like that? If Paul had met such a character he would not have been amused! Paul recalls what happened when he first shared the gospel with the Thessalonians. He had explained to them God's rescue plan to save mankind. He had described how God had sent his only Son to put that plan into operation. Now he saw that 'power' at work in his audience. It supercharged his words, making people sit up and take notice of what he was saying. He could tell that his points were hitting home and piercing deep. And the remarkable thing was that this was God's doing, not his, for he was no orator. He had no natural ability to sway a crowd through the power of his personality, or the flow of his words. The power was in the message, not the messenger. God's good news had worked a miracle in Paul's own life. Now he was the witness of a multiple-miracle. His hearers became convinced of the truth of the gospel. They felt deeply their need to ask God's forgiveness and to change their ways. And as they responded by opening their hearts, so God filled them with love, peace and joy.

There are many kinds of power. This was not brute force – destroying everything in range like the heat and blast from an H-bomb, but the power of God, personal and sensitive in its quality. It was the work of the Holy Spirit.

IT IS A TRIUMPHANT FAITH

You know how we lived when we were with you; it was for your own good. You imitated us and the Lord; and even though you suffered much, you received the message with the joy that comes from the Holy Spirit. The new believers in Thessalonica were not only well taught about the Christian life, they were shown how to live it. Watching a cookery demonstration whets the appetite far more than reading a recipe. The apostles inspired others by their way of life and dedication to Christ. And the Thessalonians learned by the apprenticeship method, watching and working under supervision.

Industry has for centuries trained its craftsmen by using this method. Night school and day-release classes can never be a substitute for years of training at the bench under the craftsman's watchful eye. The potter must learn at the wheel,

17

the wood and metal turner at the lathe, the nurse at the patient's bedside, and the Christian witness in the workshop of the world.

People soon began to notice the difference that Christ was making in the lives of the believers in this 'new religion', but they did not always like what they saw. They became uneasy, suspicious and resentful as they reacted against the things Christians were teaching and the way they lived.

The Thessalonians were given a good training. Paul showed them how to cope when people ignored them or turned against them. What is more, he taught them how to do it with the **joy that comes from the Holy Spirit**. Suffering for Christ's sake is not a punishment but a privilege, because the Jesus we follow is not a superstar but a scarred Saviour. And persecution is not just a thing of the past. There are more people in prison today for Christ than in any other period of the church's history. Baptists and Pentecostals suffer in Russia. Christian leaders and young people are massacred in Burundi. In Britain we do not face this kind of threat, but as Peter found, the sneering taunt can sometimes be more crushing than a prison sentence.

IT IS A SPREADING FAITH

. . . just like the faith of the apostles themselves. The commando missionary task force did not produce Home Guard churches! **So you became an example to all believers in Macedonia and Achaia.** The imitators were in turn imitated. **For not only did the message about the Lord go out from you throughout Macedonia and Achaia, but the news about your faith in God has gone everywhere.** The missionary outreach of these new and enthusiastic Christians in Thessalonica was spontaneous, continuous and widespread. By contrast, so often in churches today evangelism is artificial, occasional and short-lived. It is a spasm or hiccup in the life of the church, rather than its regular heartbeat.

The church in Thessalonica did not prosper through popularity. The new Christians collected more brick-bats than bouquets. But they moved ahead in the teeth of opposition. They could neither be gagged nor shouted down.

IT IS A REVOLUTIONARY FAITH

The missionaries made sure their converts had a firm grasp of basic truths, and the pupils-turned-teachers were broadcasting these without either diluting or distorting them. **There is nothing, then, that we** (the missionaries) **need to say.** As Paul and his team checked the results of the evangelistic efforts of the Thessalonians, they had to give them full marks for content plus two extra points for presentation.

The message of the gospel does more than reform – it revolutionizes.

'I never lived until I tasted . . .' runs a current vodka publicity slogan. 'People like you are changing to . . .' brashly claims a cigarette advertisement, above the minute lettering of the government health warning. But the claims of advertisers – unlike the promises of the gospel – are larger than life.

You turned away from idols to God, to serve the true and living God. Faith in Christ had made a huge difference to the way these Christians lived. They had changed from phonies to the genuine thing. It was a costly step for them to take, as government, trade, recreation and social life were all rooted in idolatry. And idolatry is no museum-piece. An idol is anything, ancient or modern, which challenges God's right to first place in our lives.

19

When we make Jesus Lord, our lives become packed with a new purpose and inspired by a bright future. With eager anticipation we **wait for his Son to come from heaven – his Son Jesus, whom he** (God) **raised from death and who rescues us from God's anger that is coming**. As the world careers along its disaster course and rushes towards the final day of reckoning, the Christian waits patiently, confident that Christ has not forgotten him. Jesus told his disciples about his return. He will come to conquer the world and set his people free. Then we will see him and be made like him. Life might seem wonderful now if we know Jesus. When he comes again, we will really understand what 'wonderful' means.

Fired with this prospect, the early church shouted with delight and longing, 'Even so, come, Lord Jesus.'

Apostles under attack

(2:1-12)

Paul and his friends were constantly under fire. In addition to rough-house tactics, there was a continuous smear campaign to blacken their characters and to discredit their motives. These slanders were particularly vicious and difficult to deal with, because Paul, the target-in-chief, was not present to defend himself. But for the sake of the gospel the charges had to be answered. Paul realized full well what his enemies were up to. By discrediting the motives of the messengers, they hoped to destroy the message itself. Every whiff of suspicion, therefore, had to be dispelled.

From Paul's reply we can reconstruct the kind of things that were being said against him. We shall see that much the same range of charges is levelled against Christians today.

THEY ARE DUDS

Their message was nothing more than hot air and old wives' tales, said the critics. It was quite irrelevant to meet the needs of today's world. When you examine it closely there is nothing there but froth and bubbles.

The Thessalonians themselves could answer that one easily enough. **Our brothers, you yourselves know that our visit to you was not a failure.** Every new believer was a living proof of the power of the gospel to change lives. Claptrap could never do that! Nor did the results stop with them. Following the example of the apostles, they were spreading the gospel far and wide. They were seeing its powerful effects in an ever-increasing number of people who were opening their lives to Jesus Christ.

THEY ARE DELINQUENTS

These strangers had arrived from Philippi as men on the run, with prison records and a lynching gang in hot pursuit. Their backs were criss-crossed with ugly weals from recent floggings. Yet they had not fled to Thessalonica in order to lie low until it was safe to operate again, nor did they attempt to conceal the facts of what had happened to them at Philippi. They had nothing to hide and no reason to be ashamed of their imprisonment and scars. **You know how we had already been ill-treated and insulted in Philippi before we came to you in Thessalonica. And even though there was much opposition, our God gave us courage to tell you the Good News that comes from him.** Nothing could silence them, whether physical torture or social disgrace.

Trumped-up charges are brought against many Christians today. Courts can be hostile and sentences harsh in lands where there is rooted opposition to the preaching of the gospel of Christ. Yet in the face of every effort to gag his witnesses and stamp out his church, Christ's servants are still given courage to speak out in the hour of need.

THEY ARE DELUDED

'If these men are not villains then they are obviously fools' – sneered their opponents – 'taken in by Jesus Christ's king-size lies.'

'Fancy being fooled into believing this incredible claim to be God's only Son and man's unique Saviour! Only an idiot can accept the planted clues as evidence that Christ had risen by evaporating through the bandages which bound his body and the solid rock which formed his tomb. These men are religious fanatics.'

Paul simply replied that **our appeal to you is not based on error**. It seems that he had carefully gone over with the Christians at Thessalonica the many prophecies from the Old Testament which had found such detailed fulfilment in Christ. Together they had sifted and weighed up the evidence of Jesus's character and claims. The evidence for the resurrection was impressive enough to stand up in any court of law. There was therefore no need for Paul to go over the ground yet again. He could dismiss the charge in a sentence.

But his opponents still had some ammunition left . . .

THEY ARE DEPRAVED

It was whispered with a smirk and a knowing wink that *impure motives* lay behind the apostles' high-sounding message. It was hinted that they were frustrated sexually and were on the prowl for weak-minded and easily influenced victims to satisfy their corrupt appetites. This line of attack was designed to link the new 'way of Christ' religion with the pagan cults which had a reputation for such goings on, and to anger the Jews who were noted for their strict moral code. A clever piece of counter-propaganda.

THEY ARE DECEIVERS

If sex was not the hidden motive of these new-style preachers, then it must be something equally sinister. No doubt they were in the gospel business for what they could get out of it in terms of power and prestige – acting in underhand ways, with the quick-sale techniques of a shop-front auctioneer, fleecing gullible people out looking for religious novelties and remedies. It was all a con-trick to line their own pockets.

Paul cannot afford to let them get away with such character assassination . . . **nor do we try to trick anyone. Instead, we always speak as God wants us to, because he has judged us worthy to be entrusted with the Good News. We do not try to please men, but to please God, who tests our motives. You know very well that we did not come to you with flattering talk.** Paul had not come with a sugar-coated message, tailoring his teaching to suit the mood of his hearers, conning them by trickery and flattery. On the contrary he had not shirked from calling a spade a spade. What he preached was raw gospel truth – that man's heart is sinful, that he has nothing with which to earn or buy his salvation, and that he must ask forgiveness.

It is impossible to adopt a 'soft sell' approach to convey the true gospel message of a suffering Saviour. And every servant of Christ must be prepared for the kind of hostile treatment that Christ himself experienced.

23

Here the critics had hit on a half-truth. As Paul puts it, 'We *could* have made demands on you.' The message he preached is one that demands everything. It represents a total way of life. Christ had appointed 'apostles' to be his special ambassadors, authorized to represent him. However, they were not to throw their weight around, seeking to build up their own position and filling their own pockets with easy pickings. It was not for themselves that they made their demands, but for God. . . . **nor did we use words to cover up greed – God is our witness! We did not try to get praise from anyone, either from you or from others, even though as apostles of Christ we could have made demands on you . . . Surely you remember, our brothers, how we worked and toiled! We worked day and night so that we would not be any trouble to you as we preached to you the Good News from God.**

In Thessalonica the pioneer missionaries earned their own keep, precisely to prevent tongues wagging with whispers of swindling. Tent-making with leather callouses the hands, strains the back and wearies the eyes. They were at it from dawn to dusk, preaching and praying as they worked.

The charge of easy money is still made against preachers. 'Be a vicar and work one day in seven. Incomprehensible on Sundays and invisible the rest of the week!' 'The church is for ever on the scrounge, yet look at the money it must have, tied up in bricks and mortar.'

Personally Paul is not over-worried by what people are saying. The only thing that really matters is that he should be approved by God in his ministry. And God's approval is not gained like a driving licence, which becomes yours for life provided your health is reasonable and you don't collect more than a few endorsements through careless or reckless action. Rather, it is given on the basis of continuous assessment – a screening which goes on for a life-time.

Family ties

(2:7, 11, 1 and 9)

Most of us can succeed in making a good impression by being on our best behaviour for special occasions. We cannot, however, fool those with whom we live. The place where truth will out is in the home, when we are relaxed, off-guard and among those with whom we are so familiar that we can be rude to them.

Paul had lived so close to these Christians at Thessalonica that he could be counted as one of the family. Although he was an apostle, there was nothing stand-offish about his manner. He had shared life with the Thessalonians. They knew about his conduct and his motives. Look at verses 1, 2, 5 and 11 for Paul's confident **You know.** He could trust them to support him, even in the witness box, because they had been open with one another. **You are our witnesses, and so is God, that our conduct towards you who believe was pure, right, and without fault.** (verse 10) There had been plenty of opportunities to weigh up these messengers of the gospel and to test their genuineness.

So Paul is sure that the Christian family will speak up for him – as he goes on to explain in family terms.

I WAS LIKE A MOTHER (v. 7)

We were gentle when we were with with you, like a mother taking care of her children. When someone with no knowledge or experience is left 'holding the baby' she is nervous and awkward. Paul and his team were wise nurse-maids. They knew how to feed, protect and bring up new believers. They were not guilty of rough handling or off-hand attitudes.

25

They are nervous and awkward.

They treated every new believer as someone important and precious, needing personal attention and loving care.

We first learn to clean our teeth by having it done for us. Then we are encouraged to hold the brush ourselves, and told how to do the job thoroughly. In the same kind of way, the young Christian grows not merely by being told, but by being shown. There are many skills in the spiritual life which need to be patiently taught and painstakingly learnt through example, correction and encouragement.

Because of our love for you we were ready to share with you

not only the Good News from God but even our own lives. (v. 8)
A bottle every four hours, washing lines always full, pram
pushing, broken nights. The whole daily routine has to be
built around baby's needs. Mother-love demands self-
sacrifice. And most mothers give themselves gladly, because
their love for their offspring is total.

There is no true spiritual sharing without self-giving, in
terms of time and effort. It may involve the draining of
emotions and nervous energy, agonies of disappointment
and patient training and correction.

Paul and his fellow-missionaries knew the pain of this
kind of love. They were not remote figures, sending out their
instructions by bush-telegraph from a plush mission HQ
hundreds of miles away. They were right in amongst the
people, speaking their language and living their life.

I WAS LIKE A FATHER (v. 11)

**You know that we treated each one of you just as a father
treats his own children.** Within the family, dad's role is
distinct from that of mum. Children are not for ever tied to
mother's apron strings. Dad is there to provide the discipline
and practical advice, so that the youngster learns to stand
on his own two feet and cope with the world around him.
It is dad who teaches us many of the everyday skills we need
to learn to be handy about the house. From his own greater
experience he is able to advise us about the path we should
take in life.

Great wisdom was needed in guiding these young believers
in Thessalonica along the path of the Christian life. They had
to learn how to react when people roughed them up or said
things that made them see red. Firm discipline was needed to
protect the newly established church and keep its standards
high. Perhaps more than anything else these young Chris-

27

. . . a fatherly word of encouragement.

tians needed to hear a fatherly word of encouragement, like
the youngster splashing and spluttering in the swimming
pool as he swims his first frantic strokes. **We encouraged you,
we comforted you, and we kept urging you to live the kind of
life that pleases God, who calls you to share in his own
Kingdom and glory. (v. 12)**

We struggle all the more when we know that we are out of
our depth. That was perhaps how the Thessalonians felt.
The gospel had brought them into a whole new way of
living. No longer were they just existing to please themselves;
they had been called to serve Christ and to live up to the
standards he set. Where this would lead they did not know.
As citizens of the Kingdom of heaven, there was nowhere
on this earth where they could go to see a working model of
God's Kingdom. They had to work at it themselves on a
trial and error basis. Theirs would be small-scale, community
efforts. But the Lord was present by his Spirit to show and
strengthen them. He was preparing them all the time for the
great day when his Kingdom would be established in full
working order.

YOU WERE LIKE BROTHERS (v. 1, 9)

As apostle, Paul was set over the new believers. He was
nursing mother, and guiding, disciplining father. But there
was a sense in which these new Christians were on a level

with him too. So he calls them 'brothers', to show that before God no one is more equal than anyone else.

'Brother' is a favourite title for believers, used twenty-one times in Paul's letters to the Thessalonians. It reminds us that we are closely related to each other. We are brothers, belonging to the same family, and not orphans who are strangers to one another, just housed together until we find a more permanent home.

But though brothers, we are not identical twins. Although we have the family likeness, we are in many respects different from one another. As brothers we are brought up together, rub off against each other, care for one another, think up schemes together, help each other out, and enjoy life together.

Thessalonians under attack

(2:13-16)

Right from the start, the church must learn to live in combat conditions. It is always outnumbered, with the outside world seeking to surround it and set up siege lines. Therefore, the church needs enormous resources and energy to survive, let alone secure a break-through. It is doomed to starve and die if its secret spiritual supply-line is cut. The apostles are overjoyed that there is not the slightest hint that the Thessalonian resistance is crumbling.

This young church's strength to survive and courage to conquer depended on two facts . . .

... we always give thanks to God. When we brought you God's message, you heard it and accepted it, not as man's message but as God's message, which indeed it is. An army commander-in-chief does not send out dispatches containing intelligence reports and orders to the forward command posts for their discussion and suggestions. He sends them out to be acted upon and obeyed. When the front-line units receive their instructions, the officers brief the senior NCOs. Soon the sergeants are shouting orders to the troops hurriedly stubbing out their cigarette ends. 'Attention! Shoulder Arms! Quick March! You there, get in step!'

The Thessalonians recognized that the message which the apostles brought was from God. The apostles were the announcers, not the authors. The Good News of the gospel is not one of man's great discoveries, nor the invention of clever preachers. It comes straight through on the hot-line from God.

But sometimes the church does not take this message at face value. It begins to ignore the bits it doesn't like and to cross out the parts it doesn't agree with. It even asks questions about the signature on the message. 'Does it really come from God?' This makes the church unsure of itself and its mission loses its drive. Today in many places the church is imprisoned in a cage of question marks. It is no longer marching ahead, and God's message is not getting through.

GOD'S WORK AMONG THEM

During a battle, when things get desperate on the fighting-front, it may become more and more difficult to carry out orders. Hard-pressed units send frantic top-priority signals to HQ asking for more men and equipment. The gospel is not only a word of command. It carries its own power-pack. Paul writes more about this in another of his letters. God's word is never hot air. It is the steam which drives the turbine.

God is at work in you who believe. The gospel is not a do-it-yourself salvation kit. It tells us that we are too weak, too stiff and unbending, and too far from home to get free and find our way back. To benefit from the gospel we not only need God's plan but his presence among us. This was the experience of Paul's readers. For them, the gospel was not about turning over a new leaf. It meant turning on to a new life.

God the Holy Spirit not only lives inside the individual Christian. He also acts through the Christian community. Local churches are like soldiers fighting a guerrilla war. They must be ready to face attacks at all times. The Holy Spirit equips them for this. He brings a unity of purpose to all the different people who make up any group of believers. He gives them the energy and the skills they need in their spiritual battles. He scouts ahead and prepares the ground for each fresh advance.

God is transmitting to his church. But if the church has its 'receiver' switched off or tuned to the wrong wavelength it will not get the message. We can only hear if we listen in. Jesus said, 'He who has ears to hear, let him hear.' If we switch off, or listen to another channel, we cannot blame God's transmitter.

The Thessalonian believers were receiving God's message loud and clear. The proof was to be found in the many ways God was active in and around them. But Paul does not play down the power of their opponents.

THE WORLD AGAINST THEM

When God is at work, the devil cannot afford to take a

holiday. In Thessalonica he had to take emergency action against the Christian activists, in an effort to block their alarming advance and break up their ranks. Their mission was too subversive to be tolerated!

The church's opponents in Thessalonica had accused the apostles of spreading a message which turned the world upside down. What they really meant was that it turned *their* world upside down. It pricked their pride too painfully. It questioned their motives too closely. And it set up an alternative way of living which they found too challenging.

Turning the world upside down? From God's stand-point it was turning a sin-twisted world the right way up.

The local opposition and persecution that had so quickly broken upon the Thessalonians was no freak storm. It is part of the regular weather pattern when the sunshine of the gospel comes into contact with the world's sin cloud-cover and the cold front of hostility and indifference.

Our brothers, the same things happened to you that happened to the churches of God in Judaea, to the people there who belong to Christ Jesus. You suffered the same persecutions from your own countrymen that they suffered from the Jews. Paul had good reason to know all about the suffering experienced by Christians in Judaea. Before his conversion he had been the very man who planned and carried out the purge against them with such ruthless thoroughness. We must keep this in mind as we read through the catalogue of crimes he lists against his own people here. The barrage of charges is the strongest blast against the Jews we find in the whole New Testament.

● **(They) killed the Lord Jesus and the prophets.** God had sent many prophets to speak to his people. They did not want to hear his word so they did not listen to his messengers. Nor did they want to hear Jesus. All through the gospels we find

32

people who were against him. Their opposition grew stronger and stronger. It bubbled like milk in a saucepan until it boiled right over. Before, they had turned away from God's prophets. Now, they went even further. They tried to silence the Lord and Saviour himself.

● . . . and persecuted us. The Jews did not call it a day after they succeeded in sending Christ to the scaffold. In the months that followed, Stephen and then James were murdered, Peter was thrown into jail and the Christian rank and file were forced to flee from Jerusalem.

● How displeasing they are to God! One of the things that displeased God most was the way the Jews dealt with his law. They added lots of detailed instructions which were originally intended merely to explain and apply the commands. In practice, it worked out differently. Their instructions grew into miles of red tape which became more important than the law itself. This man-made tradition had twisted round the law of God like a creeper, effectively strangling it.

● How hostile they are to everyone! Like a millionaire miser whose mansion overlooks a squalid shanty town, they basked in their spiritual privileges rather than face up to their responsibilities. They prided themselves on their position, and held the rest of mankind in contempt, dismissing them with a sneer as 'Gentile dogs'. And as well as rejecting the message of the Saviour whom God had sent to them, they did all they could to stop anyone else accepting him. They even tried to stop us from preaching to the Gentiles the message that would bring them salvation. This was why they stirred up the local people in Thessalonica, hired a rabble from rent-a-crowd, handed in the petition forms, and stung the authorities into action. So relentlessly had they carried through their hate campaign that Paul makes no bones about where such action will lead them. **In this way they have completed the full total of the sins they have always committed.** They had gone as far as they could go, carrying their opposition to the limit. **And now God's anger has at last come down on them!** This was self-evident in the plight of the Jews at the time of Paul's writing. God had given them up, and within a brief twenty years his wrath was let loose in the destruction of Jerusalem itself.

This was not a bad-tempered outburst on Paul's part. He is not writing from hatred but out of sorrow and concern. He is a Jew himself, proud of his family tree. He is no traitor to his people. He loves them and longs for their salvation. He looks further into the future and sees the day when the Jews will realize they have made a terrible mistake in rejecting Christ and his gospel. They will turn in sorrow, and find him with joy. You can read about these convictions regarding the future of Israel in Paul's letter to the Romans (chapters 9-11), written shortly after this one.

Out of sight, out of mind?

(2:17-3:5)

What is the church? 'Well, it's that big building on the corner, isn't it?' Is that what your answer would be? The way the New Testament describes the church is full of surprises. As well as being 'the people of God' it is pictured as 'the body of Christ' and 'the bride of Christ'. In different ways all these titles show how closely Christians are linked together, so that they feel and act as one.

They are a *body* and not just a bag of bones;

34

a *bride*, not a harem;
a *building*, not a heap of bricks.

It is not easy to work out this oneness in today's world which is far more hectic, crowded and impersonal. In the shopping centre we are surrounded by people we do not know and hardly notice. The cashier at the supermarket check-out doesn't even bother to look up as she hands us our change and trading stamps. The people at the bus stop don't smile when we join the queue.

Modern life is like switching from one merry-go-round to another. There is plenty of noise, and the movement can make us dizzy. But we get nowhere. We are caught up in the whirl of life with a lot of strangers. Even at church we can feel weary and alone. We hardly know the face of the person who sits next to us, let alone his name! It takes a great effort to speak to him.

We are cut off from one another, and this causes strain. We need to try really hard to make contact again. This is what Paul is trying to tell us here.

SEPARATION

BEING APART IS PAINFUL

As for us, brothers, when we were separated from you for a little while . . . how we missed you. We have already seen how Paul and his two helpers had been forced to leave Thessalonica. They had moved on, but only with great reluctance. With every mile they became more and more uneasy about the fate of the new believers they had left behind in the city. Although only *a little while* had passed, it must have seemed like an eternity.

This whole passage is charged with emotion. Paul had hardly had time to put names to the faces of the Christians

35

in Thessalonica, yet he cared deeply for them. He felt like a brother when war breaks up a family. He felt like a child suddenly robbed of both parents by a motorway crash (*separated* means 'orphaned'). He felt like a newly-wed parted from his bride immediately the honeymoon was over (*missed* includes the idea of 'physical desire').

Paul had arrived with his fellow-missionaries out of the blue as unknown foreigners. Their stay in the city had lasted only a few weeks. Thessalonica was just one port of call among many. They had been forced to leave in a hurry. Since then Paul had met plenty of new people and visited several new places. But his heart remained warm towards the Christians in Thessalonica. He didn't forget.

Christians are not just people who share a common interest. They enjoy a common life – eternal life given to them by Christ. And this life-bond quickly cements relationships in an atmosphere of love and trust. Within a short space of time one Christian can say to another, 'It's funny, but it seems as though I've known you all my life.'

Paul was a missionary. He *had* to get involved with other Christians. But this did not become simply a duty to be endured. For him, it was sheer delight. After all, these people were all members of his close Christian family circle. Every church service was a family reunion.

Separation hurt – but it was not complete.

When we were separated from you for a little while – not in our thoughts, of course, but only in body . . . Though distance may separate two people in love, it cannot sever their memories or feelings for each other. The Thessalonians occupied a special place in Paul's heart and were constantly in his prayers. So there was no danger of their fading from his thoughts. Here is one of the great secrets of Paul's impact on people. He had a deep and genuine concern. His converts were not scalps to be notched up, but individuals to be cared for. He felt a continuing responsibility for them.

After all, it is you – you, no less than others! – who are our hope, our joy, and our reason for boasting of our victory in the presence of our Lord Jesus when he comes. Indeed, you are our pride and our joy! Paul was a seasoned soldier on active service. He had fought spiritual battles in many places. The picture of the Thessalonians held pride of place in his gallery of memories. They were his most prized campaign medal! He not only looks back with nostalgia, but forward in joyful anticipation. He looks forward to the end of the spiritual world war. He longs for the return of Christ as the unrivalled, all-conquering Lord. He awaits the great victory procession. Then he, Paul, will proudly watch the march-past of the Thessalonians, replying to their salute. He will look along their ranks and recognize many of the faces. Each one tells a story. 'Yes, what a campaign that had been!' The thought of this triumphant reunion is enough to take some of the sting out of the present separation.

But separation can be devilishly frustrating.

How hard we tried to see you again! We wanted to return to you. I myself tried to go back more than once, but Satan would not let us. There is nothing in this letter or the book of Acts to tell us what stopped Paul from returning. Had the Town Council set up road blocks? Would Jason have lost his bond money? Had the Jews declared a Mafia-style vendetta against Paul? Was he unable to leave Athens because his diary was full of speaking engagements? We just don't know.

Whatever it was, behind all the ordinary reasons, Paul can detect the scheming of Satan. The devil is always trying to throw spanners into the missionary works. After all, every new Christian is a dead loss, as far as he's concerned. His motto is 'divide and conquer', so he continues to think up plans to separate believers, either by distance, as here, or by arguments and squabbles.

With all these diversion and 'no entry' signs it would have

37

been easy for Paul to give up all ideas of getting back to Thessalonica. But he knew he couldn't afford to call it a day. His enemies were using the loss of contact to destroy his character, and so to undermine the new-found faith of the church in Thessalonica. He had to do something.

Suddenly it dawned on him that there was a way round the road blocks which Satan had set up. If he couldn't get through himself, perhaps someone else could. Why not send Timothy?

Finally, we could not bear it any longer. So we decided to stay on alone in Athens while we sent Timothy.

CONTACT

PAYING A PRICE

The decision was a difficult one for Paul to take. The mission was risky. Timothy was a nervous and inexperienced young man. But as the junior partner and not the focus of attention, he might pass through unrecognized.

FULFILLING A PURPOSE

Despite Timothy's youth and inexperience, he had the essential qualifications for the job. Paul commends him as, **our brother who works with us for God in preaching the Good News about Christ.** Timothy was no passenger.

And his visit was not just to ease Paul's mind. The main aim of Operation Timothy was to help the church in Thessalonica. **We sent him to strengthen you and help your faith.** This was not to be a top-brass inspection, with everything put under the microscope for criticism. Timothy visited the Thessalonians as a brother, to stand beside them

38

with a message of comfort and encouragement. His ministry was a flesh-and-blood version of what the Holy Spirit was already quietly doing within their hearts.

PREVENTING A SETBACK

. . . so that none of you should turn back because of these persecutions. You yourselves know that such persecutions are part of God's will for us. For while we were still with you, we told you beforehand that we were going to be persecuted.

Paul did not suffer from a persecution complex. But Jesus had repeatedly warned his disciples to expect hostility. And Paul himself knew that Christian preachers were not always welcomed with open arms. He himself had held the coats of the men who stoned Stephen to death. He had been thrown into prison in Philippi. He had been hounded out of Thessalonica and plotted against in Berea. It was part of the price anyone had to pay for being a Christian in those times. God did not cause the persecution, but he did allow it. **You yourselves know that such persecutions are part of God's will for us.** God permits such things to happen to Christians to put their faith to the test. It is not for his benefit, but for theirs. We are all far better than we realize at deceiving ourselves about the strength of our trust in God. Opposition reveals whether our faith is simply fancy dress or protective armour.

Welcome news

(3:6-13)

Who says that the only news is bad news? That may be the general impression given by newspaper and television coverage, but it is certainly not true of the Jesus documentary. The New Testament word 'gospel' means 'good news'. Whenever we see that word in the New Testament it refers to the good news of Jesus. When he died on Good Friday and rose from the grave on Easter Day, he paid the price for our forgiveness and gave us new life. There is no better news than that!

To be more exact, we should say that this is the meaning of 'gospel' in every case except one. And the exception that proves the rule comes in Paul's words here. **Now Timothy has come back, and he has brought us the welcome news** (gospel). Paul had moved to Corinth from Athens. He was feeling very depressed and miserable when he received Timothy's wonderful news. It hit him with the full force of a gospel bombshell. He felt so delighted and relieved that it was just like getting converted all over again!

TIMOTHY REPORTS

What was there in Timothy's report from the Christians at Thessalonica? Why did it make Paul reach for his pen in such excitement?

NEWS OF THEIR *faith*

He has brought us the welcome news about your faith and love.

The church at Thessalonica was alive and well. There had been a campaign of hate. They had suffered physical torture but their faith had been proved under test conditions. The self-giving love was still there for all to see. It had neither evaporated through self-pity nor had it been poisoned by bitterness. These new Christians were still very much in business, sharing Christ's love with everyone in a spirit of joyful self-sacrifice.

NEWS OF THEIR UNBROKEN FRIENDSHIP

He has told us that you always think well of us and that you want to see us just as much as we want to see you. Attacking the message by discrediting the messenger is a familiar trick of the devil's. We still find him using it today – and sometimes with more success than he met in Thessalonica. There, he tried to force apart the new believers and the apostles who had taught them their faith. But he could not break the spirit-forged link.

Faithful preachers of the gospel are not to be treated like the pop stars in the Top Thirty – here today and forgotten tomorrow. The Thessalonians remained firmly loyal to Paul and his backing group. Far from being embarrassed by their link with public enemy No. 1 and wanting to forget all about him, they longed to have him back. They wanted the world to know that their relationship was no fair-weather friendship but an unbreakable bond. And the desire to be together again was mutual. Paul shared it too.

Among Christians, friendship runs deep.

PAUL REPLIES

The good news from Thessalonica could not have arrived at a better moment as far as Paul was concerned. In Corinth the going was tough. **So, in all our trouble and suffering we have been encouraged about you, brothers.** Just then Paul needed a boost for his morale. Yes, even the great Paul was human enough to feel down in the dumps at times. And as with us, a piece of good news helped to put the spring back in his step.

HE FELT RENEWED FOR HIS WORK

It was your faith that encouraged us. When he heard about the decisive break-through in Thessalonica, Paul took fresh heart. There was hope for Corinth too. After all, what God could do in one place he could always do in another!

Today, news of what God is doing in Latin America, East Africa, Indonesia and even nearer home helps us to believe he can do similar things where we live. If he answers our prayers for people far away, why shouldn't he answer those for the people next door?

The enthusiasm shown by Christians in other lands helps restore our flagging energy. It spurs us to renewed efforts.

HE FELT REVIVED IN HIS SPIRIT

Because now we really live if you stand firm in your life in union with the Lord. The Christian life was no part-time, leisure-hour activity for Paul. You could never describe his Christian service as in any way half-hearted. He wouldn't just go off his food for an evening if news came that the new converts in Thessalonica had stopped believing. He felt that their survival as believers was a matter of life and death to him.

The Christian race is no sprint event. It is a long-distance cross-country course, and the track is littered with obstacles.

When the new converts at Thessalonica crossed the starting line, Paul was delighted. He was just as thrilled when he heard that they were staying the course.

HE REJOICES IN HIS GOD

Now we can give thanks to our God for you. We thank him for the joy we have in his presence because of you. Success does not go to the missionaries' heads. There is no sickening self-congratulation from Paul's pen. He recognizes that all that has been achieved so far has been by courtesy of God's power. He therefore loses no time in giving him all the glory.

In particular, Paul says thank you for the joy he feels. The news had lifted him out of the doldrums. It gave him fresh heart for his work. How much we need that vital element of joy in Christian living today!

We should be prepared to share with each other.

We should be prepared to share with each other more than we do. This does not simply mean our happy experiences but our sad and painful ones as well. When our heart is light, there is a spring in our step. When we trap a finger in the door the pain shoots through our body. Paul wrote to the Christians in Corinth, 'There is no division in the body but all its different parts have the same concern for one another. If one part of the body suffers, all the other parts suffer with it; if one part is praised, all the other parts share its happiness'. (I Corinthians 12:26)

PAUL PRAYS

Timothy's good news did not prompt Paul to take the Thessalonians off his prayer list. Nor did the fact that he had to work for his keep day and night prevent him from praying day and night as well. Being busy or feeling tired is no excuse for not praying. And anyway, in addition to the many things he had to thank God for, there were still some matters which caused him concern.

Day and night we ask him with all our heart to let us see you personally and supply what is needed in your faith. Paul's delight in their progress did not blind him to the gaps in their life of faith.

If you have to criticize someone, it is always better to have it out personally. No doubt Paul would have preferred to go to Thessalonica in person. He could then have spoken to these Christians face to face. But as the chance of a visit was ruled out, at least for the time being, he knew he would have to mention these things before he put his pen down.

The players on the football field are not always the ones best able to judge the faulty tactics and detect the fouls. The expert on the touchline can see the team working as a whole, and spot the weak points, as well as the dirty play. Paul's letter is his commentary on the match so far. And one day God's action replay will reveal all!

No group of believers, no matter how alive and effective, has ever arrived spiritually. *There is always need to supply what is needed in* our *faith*. Paul asks God to do three things in particular:

HE PRAYS FOR GOD TO ARRANGE A REUNION

May our God and Father himself and our Lord Jesus prepare the way for us to come to you! Paul knows God is in control of the future. Having submitted his request for a temporary transfer he has no option but to leave the outcome in the Manager's hands. His cry here is more an urgent appeal than a threatened resignation.

Paul not only talks about prayer. He gets on with it. Prayer is as natural to him as talking. He does not have to find a special time and a private place for it. He naturally slips into praying – even in the middle of writing a letter.

But was his prayer answered? Not immediately. The Lord wanted to keep Paul out of Thessalonica for the time being. It was not until his third missionary journey that the way was opened up for him to make the longed-for return visit. Sometimes we must be prepared for God's answer to be 'Wait'.

HE PRAYS THAT GOD WILL HELP THEM TO GROW IN CHRISTIAN LOVE

Following Paul's request for himself, his second is for his Christian friends in Thessalonica. **May the Lord make your love for one another and for all people grow more and more and become as great as our love for you.**

45

The local church is to be a caring community. Its love must embrace all, giving no one the cold shoulder. It can be shown in a thousand-and-one ways. If the church fails at this point, it cannot expect to make any impact on outsiders. A cold church will receive a cold reception. Gossip and bickering are deadly diseases which attack love and readily infect any church. The love Paul refers to here is that divine love which floods the hearts of men who are in living, daily contact with God. And it is a quality of love which he does not merely preach about, but practises himself.

HE PRAYS THAT GOD WILL COMPLETE THE WORK HE HAS BEGUN IN THEM

Paul is not the power-pump of the church in Thessalonica. He does not regard himself as indispensable to their progress. It is *HE*, the Lord, who will *make your hearts strong*. It is God who put the car on the road. Paul does not then expect to have to push it along. He looks to God to supply the motor power.

. . . and you will be perfect and holy in the presence of our God and Father . . . After a certain age our bodies begin to wear out. The swimmer is at the peak of his performance in his teens. The footballer knows he will soon be hanging up his boots when he reaches his late 30s. But spiritual development is altogether different. We should progress with every passing year. We are never past our best! Every believer is capable of a top place in the first division.

One day all the faults will be removed and every scar left by sin will disappear. Then we shall conform exactly to God's design pattern and perfect standard. There will be no unfinished areas or rough edges. Each of us will stand as his masterpiece.

When will this day be? **When our Lord Jesus comes with**

all who belong to him. The world is not destined to peter out slowly. It is accelerating towards a climax. That climax will not be a big bang followed by oblivion. It will be marked by Christ's return to earth. And how different that coming will be from his first appearance. He will come in glory, accompanied by an army of dazzling angels and radiant people of God. Among them are all the great names of those who have died before his coming. When that moment comes we cannot appear shabby and ill-prepared. That day demands a lifetime's preparation, beginning now!

Marching orders
(4:1, 2)

As with many preachers, Paul's *finally* does not mean we are about to hear the full-time whistle – just that we are moving into extra time!

It also serves as a change-of-programme button. From the 'Documentary' of chapters one to three we move to the 'Do-It-Yourself' of chapters four and five.

When we glance ahead, we find a sackful of odds and ends. They cover a whole range of dos and don'ts. As the letter comes to an end, the items tumble out faster and faster. It is impossible to catch hold of them all at once.

Suddenly, this fast-moving programme is interrupted. A news flash slices into the flow of words. The armies of heaven have been mobilized. Jesus is coming. He's leading a mighty invasion force and he's about to evacuate God's people. An air-lift is beginning.

We might have expected Paul to tag the heavenly bit on at the end of his letter as the big climax. But he splits the challenge to practical living with this thunderbolt from heaven. He jolts us into realizing that Christ may come at any moment.

Life here and now is a preparation for the life to come. The timing of Christ's coming cannot be calculated. There is no suspense-building, second-by-second countdown. But come he will – there is no doubt about it!

The life of the church is not an endless serial story, with an episode every Sunday and never an end in sight. The church should not be aimlessly drifting in shifting tides and winds. It has a destination to reach, and a path to follow. The church needs clear guidance to reach its goal.

CALL TO SERVICE

. . . our brothers, you learnt from us how you should live in order to please God. This is, of course, how you have been living. And now we beg and urge you in the name of the Lord Jesus to do even more. For you know the instructions we gave you by the authority of the Lord Jesus. When Paul calls the Thessalonians *brothers* he is not appealing to them with the militant attitude of a Communist shop-steward putting across the party line. He is prompted by loving concern and not aggression.

He does not back his commands with threats. His appeal will fall on deaf ears unless it is voiced in the right way. Here are lessons on how to say what needs to be said without getting people's backs up unnecessarily.

HE SPEAKS WITH TACT

Paul issues his marching orders not as a sergeant-major but as a brother. He speaks from inside the family circle, not from outside the ranks on the parade ground. And the word of

48

command he passes on is from God – his Father as well as theirs.

Within the family we should be able to speak frankly and still remain friends. Tact is the skill of being able to touch a painful or sensitive spot in someone else's life, in the right way, at the right time.

HE SPEAKS WITH URGENCY

Tact must not be confused with timidity. Paul speaks with great feeling and urgency, **we beg and urge you**. When inexperienced sailors are struggling to keep their boat from capsizing in the teeth of a gale, the captain does not whisper suggestions, he shouts commands. Paul is aware of things which threaten to shipwreck the spiritual lives of his converts, so he makes sure that his voice is heard – loud and clear.

HE SPEAKS WITH AUTHORITY

Paul could be outspoken when the occasion demanded. It was not just because he had a 'thing' about keeping rules. Beyond the list of dos and don'ts was a God to be pleased, a person to be obeyed. And Paul speaks with his authority. **We beg and urge you** *in the name of the Lord Jesus* ... **For you know the instructions we gave you,** by *the authority of the Lord Jesus.*

Although in our New Testaments the Gospels appear before Paul's letters, they were in fact written afterwards. Until that time, Jesus's teaching was mainly passed on by word of mouth. Paul, as an apostle, was one of Jesus's special representatives, and the letters he wrote which are included in our New Testament have the same authority as Jesus's own words.

49

Paul has faith in his converts. He trusts them and praises them whenever possible. **This is, of course, how you have been living.** But just in case they are tempted to rest on their oars and pat one another on the back, he goes on to say, **do even more.** The sports coach urges his team on so that they will do even better next time. His timely words of appreciation get the most out of his men. Continuous fault-finding just wears people down. No one ever built a monument to a critic!

CONDITIONS OF SERVICE

NO FREE-WHEELERS

We cannot coast along in the Christian life, unless we are going down hill! **And now we beg and urge you, in the name of the Lord Jesus, to do** *even more.* Even our strong points need improvement.

NO PART-TIMERS

Before dealing with details, Paul speaks about what makes the Christian tick – **how you should live in order to please God.** Life cannot be divided into compartments. Christianity is not a spare-time, religious hobby. It embraces every aspect of life. Who am I living to please? Myself or God?

Men only

(4:3-8)

In Paul's day Roman society was notoriously lax with regard to sex. Wife swopping, homosexual practices, sex on demand and prostitution were all the rage. Such goings on were not confined to a small 'way out' group, but widely accepted in society.

This was the kind of world out of which the Thessalonian converts to Christ had so recently come, and in which they still had to live. When standards are at rock-bottom outside the Christian fellowship, the church can so easily be dragged down to the same level. Paul saw that a clear and firm stand was essential.

God wants you to be holy, he writes – with more than a hint of urgency. There must be no compromise. God's standards are not set by the fashions of the day, or even by church rules. When God himself speaks clearly, the Christian's duty is to fall into line, not weigh up the pros and cons. There can be no 'ifs' or 'buts'. So what does God have to say about a man's sex life?

YOUR ATTITUDE TO YOURSELF

God wants you to be holy and completely free from sexual immorality. Does this mean, 'No sex, please'?! Are we to take the vows of celibacy like monks and nuns? Are we to become frigid 'saints' of the stained-glass window variety? By no stretch of the imagination could you imagine one of them stepping out of the window arch for a kiss and a cuddle!

Holiness does not mean cutting out sex. It means coming to terms with it, so that we can value it and control it. To be 'holy' is to be 'given to God'. The Christian is someone set apart for the Lord's use. He belongs to the Lord. All of him. His body as well as his soul. And that includes his God-given urge for sex. It isn't something to be ashamed about, but accepted with thanks, and to be placed under Christ's authority. Sex is one of the most powerful instincts man has. If it gets out of control it can do a lot of damage and cause much heartache.

This is what Paul is getting at when he speaks of being **completely free from immorality**. Complete freedom does not mean an attitude in which anything goes. That is to confuse freedom with anarchy. In God's reckoning, freedom is the power to do right in place of bondage to wrong-doing. Sex out of control is lust and not love. Christ gives to the Christian the power to control his sex life so that it does not run away with him. 'Completely free' rules out week-end sexual excursions, the night-out pick-up, and flirtations by married men. Society may accept such conduct. It may be excused on the grounds of business pressure, domestic frustration, or the need to escape from the boredom of daily routine. But the Christian cannot go along with this. That road is clearly marked with a 'No entry' sign. We are forbidden to travel that way. And there is no valid reason for us to do so.

YOUR ATTITUDE TO YOUR WIFE

Sex is an exciting subject. Excitement easily results in selfishness and greed. Once the parson has said the magic words 'I pronounce you man and wife' and the reception is over, some husbands treat their new wives like dirt, in the name of love. There is more rape inside marriage than outside it.

So Paul's straight speaking is needed as much now as then.

Each of you men should know how to live with his wife in a holy and honourable way, not with a lustful desire, like the heathen who do not know God. Here Paul uses a word which can mean either 'body' or 'wife'. It is a toss-up which he had in mind. What is clear is that in the marriage relationship the husband is to regard his partner with respect as he would his own body.

The gospel dignifies the role of woman. She is no sex object to gratify personal desire. The husband is not to be demanding, forcing his favours on a reluctant partner. She is to be treated with love and sensitivity. The act of love-making means giving oneself, and not gratifying oneself.

YOUR ATTITUDE TO OTHER WOMEN

When a married man has sex with someone who is not his wife he is his own worst enemy. But the damage does not end there. No man should do wrong to his fellow-Christian or take advantage of him. This is the warning that Paul gives to the church members in Thessalonica. He was not so starry-eyed that he did not recognize the possibility of sexual misconduct amongst them. By fellow-Christian Paul has in mind the Christian who is either the husband or the father of the girl in question. The consequences of sex outside marriage reach far beyond the two who indulge in it.

WARNING

Standards of sexual conduct are a clear guide to the state of society in general. What we believe affects the way we behave. We see this in the way we behave. Anything goes. Christians have to face up to this issue. So Paul refuses to sweep any wrong use of sex under the carpet. He takes to

53

task those who injure their fellow-Christians. **We have told you this before, and we strongly warned you that the Lord will punish those who do that.** God's law contains no loopholes. It can neither be ignored nor defied.

Paul is not, however, suggesting that sexual sins are the most serious. Nor does he say that there is no forgiveness for those who fail in this area. If this were the case we would all be under condemnation. Remember Jesus said that as far as God's law was concerned the thought was as bad as the deed. A man who has not actually run off with another woman may have mentally gone to bed with her.

Christ forgives those who have gone off the rails in this matter as in any other. He welcomes us back. The past is forgotten. It is erased from God's memory. But this is no encouragement to make light of our fall. We must not trade on God's goodness by giving in a second and third time. Although we are forgiven, we have to live with the consequences of our past actions. Sin casts a long shadow. A serious wound may heal completely, but the scar can remain for life.

Paul now swings from the negative to the positive. Sin has no rightful place in the life of the Christian. It is the discordant note in a melody. It is the stain which spoils the dress. **God did not call us to live in immorality, but in holiness. So then, whoever rejects this teaching is not rejecting man, but God, who gives you his Holy Spirit.** When we persistently fail in matters of sex, we deliberately reject God's purpose for our life. We deny that the Holy Spirit has power to protect us and to help us win through. But it is never the Lord's intention that we should be underpowered. Power is restored when the engine is re-tuned to the will of God.

Living in 'Philadelphia'

(4:9-12)

Many of the people who went to North America to settle in that New World were people on the run. They were escaping from the threat of imprisonment, torture and execution in Europe. William Penn founded a city to give refuge to these people. He called it *Philadelphia*, a Greek word meaning 'brotherly love'. And this is exactly the word Paul chooses to describe the deep concern the Christians in Thessalonica felt for one another.

There is no need to write to you about love for your fellow-believers (Philadelphia). You yourselves have been taught by God how you should love one another.

EVIDENCE

Love wasn't just something the early church preached about. They practised it. In fact love was regarded as the trade-mark of genuine Christianity. Even the church's enemies whispered to themselves admiringly, 'How these Christians love one another.' By contrast today's critics sneer rather than smile when they quote those words. What was once a compliment has become a taunt.

Our twentieth-century world is far more crowded. The majority of people live in sprawling suburbs and not compact communities. We also move house and job more often. Because we don't often put down deep roots we have tended to become casual towards one another. And though the church may have many 'meetings' in its weekly programme, we do not really meet one another.

No one can work up this kind of brotherly love like a

sweat. It is quite different from the false cheerfulness of the back-slapper. It is far more than the matey feeling of being one of the gang. Love between Christians, of the kind Paul has in mind, is only possible when the divine love has first been poured into our hearts. No man can teach us to love. Only God can do that.

The Bible stresses that real love is more than a heart flutter and tingle down the spine. It shows itself in a hundred-and-one practical ways. Love drives us into making a big effort to discover the real needs of those around us. Then it moves us to do something concrete about them. Love helps us to be patient when people either bore us to tears or make us hopping mad. Love makes us sensitive to people's feelings and problems. Love prods us into good turns and generous deeds without any thought of what we might get out of it. Love helps us think the best about other people. Love kills gossip stone dead.

Others see the evidence of God's love bubbling over in the hearts of Christian people when the shut-ins are visited, the disabled brought to church, and hard-pressed single people and young marrieds helped to find accommodation, when the sick are visited and the distressed are advised and encouraged.

EXTENSION

Although brotherly love – like charity – must begin at home with one's fellow church members, it should not end there. The local church is not an exclusive club. God's love is for everyone – not just for the favoured few.

The church in Thessalonica is our great example. **And you have, in fact, behaved like this towards all the brothers in all Macedonia.** These Christians had built an extension on to their house of brotherly love. In chapter one we saw how

56

So the Christian traveller felt he belonged wherever he turned up.

their faith had been transplanted throughout Greece. Now we hear how the preachers had followed up their words by actions. And their new converts were immediately welcomed into the Christian family network. So the Christian traveller felt he belonged wherever he turned up. He could be assured of hospitality and a bed for the night.

Paul's message to the packed church in the suburbs is to look not just to their own area, but further afield. Nearby there may be struggling churches with few people and resources.

Then he might speak to them about Christian mission overseas. Perhaps they have adopted a missionary. They might even have sent one of their own members to work abroad. Are they now giving that person all the support they can? Do they pray for their missionary friend? Do they write often? Do they help in other ways? And he would prod the inward-looking church to welcome Christians from other places who have experiences and insights to share. The family of Christ is scattered throughout the world, so we need to make a real effort to keep in touch with one another. Churches, like toenails, are meant to grow outwards. In-grown toenails cause us to hobble along painfully.

EXPANSION

As always, Paul's praise never encourages Christians to pat themselves on the back. Whenever he calls out 'Great!' he also shouts 'Keep at it!' And so here. **So we beg you, our brothers, to do even more.** Even our strong points are capable of further improvement. We are never in a position to sit back and rest upon our laurels. The Christian life is a marathon, not a sprint.

Once more the amber warning light flashes on. When Christian people are deeply concerned for one another and sharing generously with each other, then some individuals take advantage of the situation. It might be immediately or some time later. Paul introduces us to some of the problem people and shows us how to deal with them.

To the *fanatic* Paul says, 'Don't get worked up,' **make it your aim to live a quiet life.** Some believers were obsessed with the idea that Christ would be returning to earth in the very near future. He had gone to heaven to prepare their homes and before long would be coming to collect them. Therefore it wasn't worth getting involved in anything down here at this late stage. They were all ready to go. Their bags were packed and they were in the airport lounge. They were standing about, chatting excitedly. They expected their flight to heaven to be called at any minute.

Paul keeps them firmly grounded. He tells them to calm down. They cannot escape the dull routine of life. They must learn to see the Lord's hand in everyday affairs and to serve him faithfully in humdrum jobs.

To the *busybody* Paul says, 'Don't be nosey,' **mind your own business.** We are all prone to become collectors of juicy titbits of information which we trade around the church's gossip group, piously disguised as prayer topics. When anyone takes us into their confidence we must take great care not to break their trust. Confidences should never be paraded or dragged into the open by the probings of un-healthy curiosity.

To the *layabouts* Paul says, 'Don't sponge on others,' **earn your own living.** The early church showed its practical care for those in material need. But it didn't encourage people to live for ever on the dole. The fellowship must take steps to ensure that its aid programme does not result in the breeding of social parasites, of people no longer prepared to get their hands dirty. The object is not to provide splints for lame ducks, but to give them an opportunity to get back into the swim.

This down-to-earth advice is only a repetition of what Paul had said during the course of his visit. **Just as we told you before.** Some lessons are hard to learn. It is understandably easy to become hard-hearted through being 'conned' or taken advantage of by so-called Christian brothers. However, such unpleasant experiences should make us wiser and not harder.

EXAMPLE

In this way you will win the respect of those who are not believers, and you will not have to depend on anyone for what you need. The church establishes its reputation by the quality of its life. It will make or break its image to the extent it succeeds in acting on the down-to-earth matters raised in this chapter. Are we laying ourselves open to accusations of being work-shy, clock-watchers and cadgers?

The royal reception
(4:13-18)

You are caught up in a whirl of excitement. You have just received an invitation to a reception at Buckingham Palace. Eagerly you plan what you will wear and then off you go on a spending spree to buy your new outfit. You arrange for transport and check and double check all the details. In a thrill of anticipation you let your mind turn over all that could happen. Then tragedy strikes. You fall. You break your leg. You are confined to a hospital bed. The red-letter day arrives and you are not there.

Paul had taught the new believers about the certainty of Christ's return to earth. It was a subject dear to his heart and often on his lips. His converts had caught his enthusiasm. As they thought of the future, the prospect of Christ's coming filled their horizon. And they expected it any day.

But when Timothy returned to Thessalonica he found some of the Christians there deeply distressed. The cause of the sadness was that one or two of their number had died, and their Christian friends thought that their passing meant that they would miss out on the celebrations when Christ returned. Many of these new Christians had been pagans, and for the pagan death comes with a fearful finality. At the worst it spells extinction, and at the best agonizing uncertainty.

No doubt Timothy was able to clear up their misunderstanding. Yet Paul wants to make absolutely sure. The subject is too important to leave to chance. So just in case any of the Thessalonians are still uncertain or muddled in their thinking, he puts on record some clear teaching about the believers who have died. He writes to reassure them. Those who have died before Christ's return will not miss out. No calamity will rob the Thessalonians of their seats at the Lord's victory celebrations. There will be no broken legs there.

THE SLEEPERS

Our brothers, we want you to know the truth about those who have died. Perhaps the Thessalonians thought that their friends' deaths were due to punishment for sin. If so, Paul shows how mistaken they are. God has neither banished nor exterminated those who have died. The believer who has passed from this life is with Christ now and will accompany him on his return. . . . **We believe that God will take back with Jesus those who have died believing in him.**

THE SORROWFUL

To those who mourn, Paul offers comfort. He explains that death for the Christian is no terrifying leap into a black pit, but a gentle step into eternity. We are told for sure on this side of the grave of a heavenly welcome on the other. To underline the point the word he uses for 'died' means 'asleep'. **We want you to know the truth about those who have died (fallen asleep) so that you will not be sad as are those who have no hope.** Sleep is natural and holds no terror. When the body is tired and worn, rest is welcome.

Some people think that this passage about 'sleep' means that Christians will experience nothing until the resurrection day. This, however, may be pressing Paul's word's too far. The important thing to be sure about is that from the moment we leave this life we are with Christ.

For the Christian there can be gladness even at the graveside, because every believer can be absolutely sure of life after death. This confidence does not rest on pious hope or the 'voices' of mediums, but on solid historical fact. It is based on what happened to Jesus. **We believe that Jesus died and rose again, and so we believe that God will take back with Jesus those who have died (fallen asleep) believing in him.** Christ has conquered death. The stone was rolled away from the tomb. It was not to let Christ out but to let people in. They could see for themselves what had happened. The empty grave clothes proved that it was not just his spirit

62

which revived, but his body which arose. He has opened up the way to heaven. He has prepared the reception centre. And when he returns to earth he will bring with him all believers who have died.

When the first astronauts had landed on the moon and returned to tell the tale, others could then follow with confidence. After Christ rose from the dead, he returned to his followers. They saw him and heard him speak. They touched him and ate with him. In these ways, he reassured them.

THE SURVIVORS

Paul now turns his attention on those who are alive at the time of Christ's coming. Hopefully he says, 'we who are alive'. He longed for Jesus to come soon. He cannot give any date, because he just does not know. But every day he was ready and prepared.

● The survivors will have to wait their turn.
What we are teaching you now is the Lord's teaching: we who are alive on the day the Lord comes will not go ahead of those who have died ... Those who have died believing in Christ will rise to life first. Christians who have died will be first in the queue! Those who have died believing in Christ are with him now, and are awake to the fact. But they too await the great day of Christ's return to earth, because then they will receive their 'new life' bodies. These will not be phantom versions of the flesh and blood bodies they had here on earth. In fact our earthly bodies are just temporary versions of the real bodies we will receive!

● The survivors will hear a noise that will rivet their attention.

There will be the shout of command, the archangel's voice, the sound of God's trumpet, and the Lord himself will come down from heaven. Heaven's liberation army will take over the world. The invasion and the victory will coincide. The voice of command and the bugle call are the signal for Christ's triumphant descent.

As we picture these events we must not just take them at their face value. The events themselves defy description. Paul is giving us the atmosphere. It is more of a poem than a programme. The essential truths to grasp are that Christ is coming again, he is coming in triumph, and no one will be left in any doubt when the moment comes.

● The survivors will be air-lifted into Christ's presence. **Those who have died believing in Christ will rise to life first; then we who are living at that time will all be gathered up along with them in the clouds to meet the Lord in the air.** This will be the greatest reunion of all times. It does not mean that we will recapture the past with nostalgia, like a gathering of war veterans. Instead we will step together into a glorious and endless future. And heaven is not a place of countless cubicles with each door marked 'private'; it is a place where Christians will be together and sharing with each other at far deeper levels than they have known on earth.

And so we will always be with the Lord. We can prepare for this glorious future now. We must get to know Jesus well here on earth. Our lives must show that we trust him with confidence and obey him in love.

We began this passage stooping gloomily at the graveside. We end it, standing on tip-toe eagerly straining for the glimpse of Christ's coming. **So then, encourage one another with these words.**

Battle stations

(5:1-11)

The air forces of the major powers are in a state of constant readiness. Radar beams scan the skies around the clock. Missiles appear from their underground silos at the touch of a button. Pilots sit in the cockpits of their fighter interceptors ready for instant take-off on the word of command from the control tower. In modern warfare every second counts.

From time to time this state of readiness is tested by high command. When the warning lights begin to flash, and the vital code-words are released, no one outside HQ knows whether it is just another exercise or the real thing.

The army of Christ in Thessalonica is fully mobilized and

The army of Christ in Thessalonica is fully mobilized.

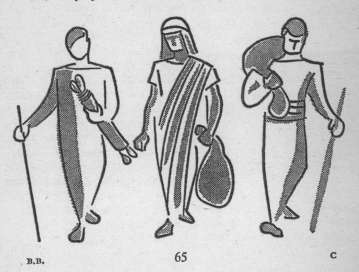

already grappling with the enemy. But the global clash is still to come. They know that their local battles are just part of the build-up leading to the final conflict and ultimate victory. **There is no need to write to you, brothers, about the times and occasions when these things will happen.** Paul is a master of strategy where missionary work is concerned. He looks ahead to the climax of the campaign. Christ will demand the unconditional surrender of all that is evil. Then he will stage his victory parade. Paul is fully informed of the state of readiness of the church in Thessalonica. He is confident that they will not be taken by surprise. They have their early-warning system in operation, and their manpower is combat trained and fully mobilized.

FOREWARNED

The coming of Christ will be sudden, without warning. Zero hour is unknown, with no possibility of a security leak!

LIKE A ROBBERY

For you yourselves know very well that the Day of the Lord will come as a thief comes at night. When people say, 'Everything is quiet and safe,' then suddenly destruction will hit them! Christ's D-day might mean liberation for the people of God. It will mean judgement for those who have turned their backs on him. Throughout the centuries such an idea has been generally laughed at. The solemn warning, 'Prepare to meet thy God,' on the back of a sandwich-board causes more amusement than terror. 'It could never happen to us,' people say – just like the housewife who leaves the front door on the latch and is surprised to find the colour television gone when she gets back from her shopping.

Satan's strategy is to lull the world into a sense of false security. He makes the day of reckoning seem unlikely and remote. We look back at the centuries which have passed, and imagine that there is an equal amount of future still to come. Strange to say, in recent years it has been the scientists rather than the church who have been sounding the warning bells.

LIKE LABOUR-PAINS

It will come as suddenly as the pains that come upon a woman in labour, and people will not escape. Near the end of the nine months' pregnancy the mother-to-be expects her baby at any moment. As zero hour approaches, so the contractions begin. She asks herself, 'Is it a false alarm, or the real thing this time?' Now the pains become more regular and intense. This is it! Call the hospital! Once in the labour ward it is only a matter of hours before the baby is delivered. To her anxious husband pacing up and down at home it may seem an eternity.

There is no putting off the Day of the Lord. Once the signs start to appear events will follow one on top of another. There is no escaping the consequences. Everyone must see the whole thing through from beginning to end. The Lord's coming will result in a life-and-death struggle here on earth. This is why Paul's illustration of childbirth is so appropriate. In his day, giving birth was a much more hazardous event.

FOREARMED

In view of the instant-alert situation in which we live we need to be ready all the time. A spiritual war is being waged. Christ's soldiers must sleep with their boots on.

. . . for the day has dawned, reveille has sounded. **All of you are people who belong to the light, who belong to the day. We do not belong to the night or to the darkness. So then, we should not be sleeping, like the others; . . . It is at night that people sleep.** Those without Christ live in darkness. They are spiritually asleep. They will not answer at all when God's urgent call comes. For Christians, however, the darkness of sin has been broken by Christ's light. Their eyes have been opened to realize that it is day, and they must get up, for there is much to do.

It is doubly difficult to rise early in the morning when the rest of the family are in bed! How strong is the temptation to doze off again! So the sleeping church needs to hear a loud alarm. It rings not only from the pages of the Bible but from events on our doorstep and around the world. The first person awake must rouse the rest of us. Then together we must do all in our power to stir the world.

ALERT

We should be awake and sober. It is at night that they get drunk. A man on guard duty who is sozzled is not only useless, he is a menace to the rest. His mind is befuddled, his vision blurred, his speech slurred and his walk unsteady. He can neither get a grip on himself nor grasp what is going on around him. Paul reminds Christians that pub-crawling is an after-work, night-time activity. But Christians work around the clock. Because of this they need a clear head and steady hand at all times. The church is always on the road. So if you drink be careful how you drive – keep the alcohol level down to within safe limits! Excesses of any kind make the church unreliable in its performance.

We must wear faith and love as a breastplate, and our hope of salvation as a helmet. Paul must have been very familiar with the uniform of the Roman soldier. He often uses it as a visual aid in his letters. Perhaps he had grown up with a picture of a soldier on the wall. Here he gives us just a thumb-nail sketch of the fighting man's two most important items of protective equipment. Perhaps he is worried that the Thessalonians, flushed with their recent triumphs, may be neglecting their defences. These items of combat kit are to be worn at all times, for we are never safe from sniper fire. When Satan prepares to attack he takes careful aim at either our heart or our head. These are the most vital parts of the body. He goes for the heart to make us hard, instead of loving. He attacks the head to make us depressed, instead of alive with hope.

The Thessalonians were already showing that their armour gave effective protection. It was being tested during close combat in a tough battle. Remember what Paul says at the beginning of his letter? He rejoices that the Thessalonians are putting their faith into practice. He is happy that their love is making them work so hard. Above all, he rejoices that their hope in the Lord Jesus is firm.

ASSURED

BY THE FACTS

God did not choose us to suffer his anger, but to possess salvation through our Lord Jesus Christ, who died for us in order that we might live together with him, whether we are alive or dead when he comes. For believers there is no doubt about the final outcome. Neither the doom prophets of science, nor the cosmic chaos and divine judgement foretold by the Bible, need hold any terror for them.

If we go abroad, we need a passport. The Christian travels with the necessary documents to see him safely through this life and into the next. He carries a free pardon for his past wrong-doing. Jesus died for him on the cross at Calvary. He secured the forgiveness a sinner needs.

He also carries a diplomatic passport. It says he is a citizen of Christ's kingdom. What is more, it shows that he is in constant touch with his sovereign.

BY THE FELLOWSHIP

As Christians we look forward to the future, not with fear but with a guaranteed hope. **And so encourage one another and help one another, just as you are now doing.** It is dangerous to get cut off from your combat unit when the battle hots up and the enemy is at close quarters. Paul tells us to keep together. He reminds us of our duty. We should always be ready to boost morale and to help each other. We are instructed to fight side by side. If we break rank, we expose the rest. Team work and team loyalty are essential. Paul is so thankful to see these qualities in action in Thessalonica. He encourages his friends to keep up the good work.

Leaders and stragglers

(5:12-15)

When the wife is going away for a few days, leaving the family in the care of the husband, the last moments before her departure are filled with a shower of instructions. 'Don't forget to tell the milkman three pints instead of four . . . Get a chicken for the week-end . . . Jimmy needs his medicine at 9 a.m. and 6 p.m. . . . Make sure to put the cat out.'

This is the pace of the concluding sentences of this letter. Either Paul must be running out of time, or his scroll is coming to an end. Like a modern airmail letter there is no room for extra pages. Everything has to be crammed into the space available. So after some quick words of advice on treating church leaders with the respect they deserve, he turns his attention to the stragglers who bring up the rear.

RESPECT FOR THE LEADERS

We beg you, our brothers, to pay proper respect to those who work among you, who guide and instruct you in the Christian life. Treat them with the greatest respect and love because of the work they do. Remember, the church in Thessalonica was only months old. Paul's stay had been all too brief, and the instruction he had been able to give these new converts was only a crash course. No experienced missionary had been left in the city to care for them. There was no neighbouring Bible college turning out ready-made leaders. The local leadership could not be imported. It had to be home-grown.

As the church is discovering, in some parts of the world today, there are both advantages and disadvantages in this

71

system of do-it-yourself leadership. In the first place it is cheap and flexible. Both these are essential in a fast-growing first-generation missionary situation.

Another bonus is that when a man is trained on the job, learning by doing, he never loses contact with the people among whom he has grown up. His ministry will be all the more relevant to them. He is more likely to scratch where they itch.

On the other hand, there are problems. Paul touches on one of them here – *lack of respect*. The leader's fellow-Christians know that he is just one of them. They have grown up with him. They have worked alongside him. They may, therefore, kick against his authority. Everybody wants to be a sheriff rather than a cowboy.

It happens today. In Chile, for example, there are between 80 and 125 legally recognized Pentecostal groups. It is not doctrine which has caused the divisions. Instead, in most cases, it is the struggle for power in local churches which has split the main body. Paul writes to prevent such a thing happening in Thessalonica.

The newly-appointed church leaders are not there to look pretty but to do a job. They are to be respected not so much for who they are, but (in Paul's words) *because of the work they do*. In an army an officer is saluted in recognition of the commission that he holds. It must be the same in the church.

What is this job that church leaders are appointed to do?

THEY ARE LABOURERS

When Paul says 'work' he has physical exertion in mind. The Christian ministry involves sweat and toil. This is a reminder to those honoured with the responsibility of leadership that they are not to lord it over the rest. They are not to tell other people to do what they are not prepared to

72

do themselves. You cannot lead a church from behind an office desk. You cannot use the pulpit as the captain's bridge from which orders are shouted to the 'crew' on the deck below. The leader must work alongside. He must be prepared to roll up his sleeves and bend his back as well as use his brain.

THEY ARE FOREMEN

Leaders are there to 'guide' – to show the way and set the example. This does not mean that they must be jack-of-all-trades. Paul is not thinking of a one-man-band. He is thinking of a leadership team. The Christian leader's task is not to run the whole show. He must work with others and help them to find their place and make their contribution. He is like the player-manager of a football team. The individual players have the flair and the skills. He must weld them together and use and develop their talents. He must build up strategic attacking and defensive moves. Good team work results in the right men being in the right place at the right time.

THEY ARE TROUBLE-SHOOTERS

Our English word 'instruct' does not have the full force of the word Paul himself used. As well as 'teach', he meant 'tick off' when the occasion demanded. There must be a willingness to give and take correction within the local church. The leader must not be high-handed and harsh when he reprimands others and the church member must not be too touchy to accept this kind of discipline.

Be at peace among yourselves. Paul finishes his words about leadership with a sound piece of advice. There must be no jockeying for power, no rival splinter-groups and no arm-chair critics.

REGARD FOR THE STRAGGLERS

The spiritual pace was fast in the church in Thessalonica. Christians were expected to live up to high standards of behaviour. They were called upon to make great efforts in their Christian service. Many were eager to share their new-found faith far and wide. Perhaps for some this seemed like an uphill struggle and they were having difficulty in keeping up with the main body.

Paul does not just leave it to the leaders to deal with the stragglers. He writes, **We urge you, our brothers, to warn the idle, encourage the timid, help the weak, be patient with everyone.** For a variety of reasons, the church which is going places finds that the column thins out. Those at the front may forget that there are those at the back limping along so slowly that they are in danger of losing contact entirely. The church is like a bath. It is no good having water coming in through the tap if even more is escaping through the plug-hole. Stragglers must be helped – this is the message Paul spells out in as much detail as space allows.

Warn the idle. 'You there! Get in step! Or I'll tear your arm off and hit you over the head with the soggy end!' yells the parade-ground sergeant at his odd-man-out. Paul in his choice of words shows that this is the kind of picture he has in mind. The man out of step is a menace to the rest. He can quickly have the whole parade in disarray. Often there are those who want to go their own way. There may be others who deliberately drag their feet. If the fellowship is to stick together, it is sometimes necessary to tick these people off.

Encourage the timid. On the other hand we must be careful not to snuff out the flickering fire with the gale-force wind of enthusiasm. Spiritual supermen can too easily write off the timid as spineless and useless. Young Timothy, whose name Paul links with this letter, was a quiet, nervous man. But Paul practised what he preached. He took Timothy in hand, entrusted important errands to him, put him firmly in the firing line, and eventually placed a whole group of churches in his care.

Help the weak. Some people are weak-willed. They can never say 'No'. This sometimes leads them into one mess after another – HP debts, work fiddles, gambling, heavy drinking and so on. Others are weak, not through their own fault, but due to circumstances beyond their control. There is the parent who is unable to cope with the family after being abandoned by a partner or bereaved. Then we find the sick person unable to work or look after the home any longer or the disturbed person unable to relate to people and keep down a regular job. Still others are weak in the sense that they feel helpless to get a grievance aired or a problem sorted out and they need a spokesman to represent them before the appropriate authority.

Casualties are not to be callously abandoned to a merciless enemy. The fellowship of the church cares lovingly for those who are in difficulties. We must stick by the weak, assisting them along at the best pace they can manage.

Be patient with everyone. Just because we are so different, it is easy to rub one another up the wrong way. For one reason or another we can write everybody off. 'All the world's daft save thee and me, and even thee's a bit queer,' runs the Yorkshire saying. Patience involves tolerance. It means making a real effort to understand and accept the person who is different in temperament and outlook from ourselves.

When we get hot under the collar and on the verge of exploding, we must remember that Jesus made it quite clear that hitting back is out. Paul here makes the same point. **See that no one pays back wrong for wrong.** There must be no bearing of grudges. Sometimes when we say we have buried the hatchet we leave the handle sticking out ready to grab when no one is looking. **But at all times make it your**

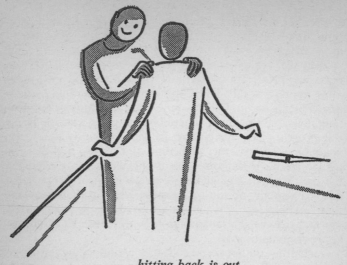

. . . hitting back is out.

aim to do good to one another and to all people. This is the positive command. Warm-hearted generosity and sensitive caring should be the trade-marks of a church.

Over and out

(5:16-28)

Paul's letter ends with a string of instructions, which judder out like ticker-tape messages. There is no particular order, so we will refrain from trying to impose one. We'll just read off the clipped phrases as they leave the teleprinter.

STANDING ORDERS

... BE JOYFUL ALWAYS ... PRAY AT ALL
TIMES ... BE THANKFUL IN ALL CIRCUM-
STANCES. Here are three permanent characteristics of
the Christian's life and the church's fellowship. Our joy does
not stem from the fact that we are living in clover, but from
our living in Christ's love. When Paul was writing it was
tough going both for the converts in Thessalonica and for
him in Corinth. Yet he could urge the Thessalonians to be
joyful. This was because he and they shared in the forgiveness which comes from the heavenly Father. They knew the
presence of Christ because his Spirit lived in them. They
were supported by fellow-believers and they had a fabulous
future to look forward to. Their joy was the delight they felt
in all this.

While our feet must be firmly planted on earth, our hearts
are to be in heaven. Prayer is the Christian's language of the
heart. Paul punctuates his letters with prayer, for he is
utterly dependent on the presence and power of God at
every turn. As a mature servant of God he makes frequent
use of the hot-line to heaven. Great damage can so easily be
done when we rely merely on our own wisdom and strength.
'Life is fragile – handle with prayer.'

It is unrealistic to be thankful *for* all circumstances. Sometimes terrible things hit our lives. But we can learn to be
thankful *in* all circumstances. We know God has the last
word. He is in ultimate control. Events are never allowed to
get out of hand. God may permit sickness, an exam failure,
a redundancy, a bankruptcy, a broken engagement. Even
when we do not understand his reasons for allowing such
things we must trust him, for he is a loving heavenly Father.
All that he does, or allows, is for a good purpose. It may be
to increase our faith, or to get our priorities right. He may
want to steer us away from some course of action which

77

would lead to catastrophe. Whether we see the reasons or not, we can trust his judgement.

Gladness, not gloom; prayer, not worry. Thanks. **This is what God wants from you in your life in union with Christ Jesus.**

FIRE PRECAUTIONS

DO NOT RESTRAIN (EXTINGUISH) THE HOLY SPIRIT...DO NOT DESPISE INSPIRED MESSAGES . . . PUT ALL THINGS TO THE TEST: KEEP WHAT IS GOOD, AND AVOID EVERY KIND OF EVIL. When the fire of the Spirit is fanned by the wind of the Spirit, it is wrong to spoil things by trying to put it out. The Spirit of God is not a destructive, brute force. He comes as fire for good reasons. He burns up the rubbish that clutters our lives. He gives light when we don't know where to turn next. He provides warmth when we are chilled by discouragement. The first precaution then, is 'Don't be a wet blanket'. Instead, add fuel to God's fire.

God is present in the lives of his people by his Holy Spirit. He may move them at any time to do and say things which do not appear in black and white on the church's programme card. He brings a delightful variety and spontaneity to church life. In Corinth, where Paul sat writing this letter, all kinds of exciting things were happening. But there the spiritual firework display was in danger of getting out of hand. Here, in Thessalonica, the problem was just the opposite. Frightened church people were pouring buckets of cold water on the Spirit's fire in the hope of avoiding any uncomfortable explosions. Paul gives a specific instance. **Do not despise inspired messages.**

Since way back in Old Testament times, God had revealed his will to some of his servants who then shared the inspired message with the rest of his people. These spokesmen for God were called prophets. And God had his prophets in the New Testament church too. Through their inspired messages, he set about guiding his church. So why were there some in Thessalonica who wanted to silence the prophets' voices? The answer, perhaps, is that just like us they didn't want to be told to pull up their socks, or take on anything extra, or stand down for someone else. If they did anything, they wanted it to be on their own terms rather than God's.

When a prophet speaks a true word from God there can be no ifs and buts. We have to knuckle under to get on with it.

Paul himself had been suddenly uprooted through a prophet's message. He was in Antioch at the time and the Holy Spirit spoke to the congregation as they were at prayer. 'Set apart for me Barnabas and Saul, to do the work to which I have called them.' The church did not respond by protesting that they could not possibly spare their two best men. They did not delegate the job to others. Nor did they try delaying tactics. 'They fasted and prayed, placed their hands on them and sent them off.' (See Acts 13:3)

There is an important difference, of course, between being responsive and being gullible. When you buy a bottle of aspirin it says on the bottle 'B.P.C.' This means British Pharmaceutical Codex. It tells you that the drug has been tested. You can be sure that the tablets are what they claim to be and that they contain the minimum of impurities. In the same way every message and action which it is claimed comes from God needs to be tested. It may have a purely human explanation. It may even be the work of the devil. So alongside the gift of faith we need spiritual insight to sort out what is genuine from the phoney. The sifting operation will lead to the accepting of some things and to the rejecting of others. **Keep what is good and avoid every kind of evil.** We are to follow the message if it conforms to certain rules.

It should correspond with God's written word, the Bible. We can be guided by the writings of the apostles which we call the New Testament. We can also learn from the Old Testament. Then we should also be sure deep down inside that it agrees with God's character. The Holy Spirit never tells us to do anything that is morally wrong.

OWNERSHIP

Once more Paul plunges into prayer, for he knows the Thessalonians need more than orders from him. They also need the reassurance of God and his controlling hand upon their lives. **May the God who gives us peace make you holy in every way.** This is a flash-back to the greeting at the beginning of the letter. Peace means completeness and inward prosperity. And God's peace can only come when our lives are wide open to the influence of his Spirit. Then he can make and keep us spiritually clean. **Keep your whole being – spirit, soul, and body – free from every fault at the coming of our Lord Jesus Christ.**

It is only God who can prevent us from becoming stale and feeble. All our powers are to be yielded to him – intellectual, emotional and physical – so that nothing goes missing or begins to go wrong. If we place ourselves completely in his hands there is no need to be uncertain or anxious about the future. **He who calls you will do it, because he is faithful!**

PRAYER PARTNERSHIP

The fact that Paul is a compulsive pray-er does not mean that he thinks himself above the need for other people's prayers. **Pray also for us, brothers,** he asks. Prayer partnership is a two-way commitment. Members of the local church should pray for one another. Every church should show its missionary concern by praying regularly and personally for Christian groups with which it is linked in other parts of the country and of the world.

SHOWING AFFECTION

Greet all the believers with a brotherly kiss. The very thought makes most Anglo-Saxons shudder! Kissing and cuddling might be OK for Frenchmen, Russians and Latin Americans but it's not very British. Of course, people of different cultures greet one another in different ways. Presumably, if Paul had been writing to Eskimos he would have said, 'Greet all the believers with a brotherly nose-rub.' And if he'd been writing to Britons he would have said, 'Give each other a hearty handshake!' There is something wrong with us when even the thought of greeting one another and shaking hands in church is enough to make us come out in goose pimples. Many Christians need freeing from the phobia of physical contact. In how many of our 'meetings' do we really meet? As Christians we cannot ignore one another, or just give a casual nod. However we do it, we are to greet one another affectionately.

SPREADING THE WORD

I urge you by the authority of the Lord to read this letter to all the believers. Paul puts the church leaders in Thessalonica under oath to read his letter to the whole congregation. And they weren't to serve it up week by week like little squares of chocolate to make the bar last as long as possible! It was designed to be read at one sitting.

Most of Paul's letters can be read right through in a space of ten minutes to half an hour, depending on the length. We can lose some of the atmosphere if we only hear them read in short bursts on Sundays.

Paul ordered the church leaders to read his letters to all the members of God's family because it applied to everybody without exception. He expected them to respond, not just by saying 'How nice of Paul to drop us a line' but to agree to take action on all the points which he had raised.

SIGNING OFF

The grace of our Lord Jesus Christ be with you. Phew! What a lot to think about! We are going to need an enormous amount of help to put it into practice. Paul is well aware of our need and points us to the Lord who alone can supply it. *Grace* is his outstretched hand – to welcome us, to lift us up, to comfort us, to protect us, to push us along and to guide us every step of the way. The risen Lord says to us as he said to Paul, 'My grace is sufficient for you, for my power is made perfect in weakness.'

2 Thessalonians

For better or for worse

(1:1, 2)

When the bride and the bridegroom stand hand in hand at
the altar rail they take each other 'for better or for worse'.
They hope it will be the first rather than the second. But
when you commit yourself for life you must be willing to
take the rough with the smooth. So the wedding service
makes a couple in love face the plain facts of life. It takes up
the documentary where the fairy tale ends. It adds the real-
life touches to the romantic picture of the beautiful young
maiden who marries her handsome prince, and walks hand
in hand with him into a golden sunset to live happily ever
after.

In the real world the road of life is sometimes rough and
steep. It has many ups and downs, pitfalls and switchbacks.
Families have to learn to cope with the strains and stresses,
the disappointments and failures. Difficult times either pull
members of the family together or tear them apart. They
have to try to be understanding and forgiving. They have to
learn to be patient with one another. Things don't always
work out as we had hoped or planned. If our family life
means anything to us, we have to accept this. We are committed to one another 'for better or for worse'. So we cannot
just up anchor and sail away!

The same is true for the family of Christ.

Paul's first letter to the believers in Thessalonica had not
done what he had hoped it would do. Now he felt he had to
write another. No matter how clearly one tries to write, some
people will always succeed in getting the wrong end of the
stick. And then there are those who will only hear the bits

that they want to hear. They quickly skip over the painful truths they need to learn most. Letter-writing can be a frustrating business.

Paul's letters to the Thessalonians are not of the formal, business kind. They are written from one member of the family to the rest. They are the kind that end 'with love', not 'yours faithfully'. As we have seen, the first was written in Corinth and taken by Timothy to Thessalonica. A reply then reaches Paul while he is still in Corinth. At this stage in their life the Thessalonian Christians need Paul's guidance badly. It is good that he remained in this city for eighteen months. This meant he was close enough to them not to lose touch altogether.

Unfortunately Paul did not date his letters and there is no envelope bearing a postmark. If we want to know when these two letters were written we have to do some complicated guess-work. By slotting the New Testament book of Acts into Roman history of the period, we can work out roughly when Paul was where. His stay in Corinth can be fixed at around AD 50 or 51. This is the period when 1 and 2 Thessalonians were written. They appeared within a few months of each other.

These letters are almost certainly the earliest of Paul's writings to be found in the New Testament. They were in the hands of these first Christians before they had any gospels. The gospel writers' accounts of the life and teaching of Jesus began to appear a few years later. This helps us to realize why misunderstandings arose so easily. The early Christians couldn't look Jesus up in a book. They had to learn all they knew from the apostles and other travelling witnesses. No wonder Paul's letters were so important to them. Most of them had nothing else in writing at all.

Like the last letter this one begins with the names of the three men who signed it. **From Paul, Silas, and Timothy.** Paul wrote it, but the other two wanted to be included. Like the three legs of a stool they all supported the new believers in Thessalonica. They would not let them down.

It was easy enough to pick faults with the beliefs and lives of the Thessalonians. Like a new car they needed running in and adjustments made here and there. No one ditches a roadworthy vehicle at the first sign of trouble. The owner takes it to the garage for a skilled mechanic to look under the bonnet and check the different parts. So Paul's aim here is to give the church at Thessalonica a second servicing.

He goes about the job coolly and skilfully. There is no danger of his throwing a spanner through the windscreen in despair. Things don't always work out right first time. His motto is, if at first you don't succeed then try and try again.

THEY WERE ORDINARY PEOPLE

To the people of the church. They had switched on to Paul's preaching, and under the world's searchlight gaze, they had stepped forward for Jesus Christ. It took real guts to make a move of that kind. They could not have done it without God's prompting and power. Yet for all that, they did not spring up as instant super-Christians. They all had their weaknesses and blind spots. They were not plaster saints but flesh and blood people. Paul knew many of them personally. He wouldn't look at them through rose-tinted glasses. So when they stumbled or fell he did not become impatient or lose heart. He simply picked them up, dusted them down, and set them on their way again.

THEY LIVED IN A DIFFICULT PLACE

To the people of the church in Thessalonica. Paul's first letter left us in no doubt as to the kind of place Thessalonica was.

It was certainly no seaside health resort for jaded Christians. Believers did not go there to bask by the blue Aegean. Imagine holding a Christian convention in Moscow, Peking or Ho Chi Minh City today! First-century Thessalonica was just as unlikely. It was a tough place to wear Christ's badge in your button-hole. And if you did, unpleasant things were likely to happen to you. Apart from the threat of physical violence, there was a constant undercurrent of criticism and sinister whispers. It is difficult to live in that kind of atmosphere. It sets the nerves on edge. At such times, it helps to have friends, even if they are far away. You can at least count on their concern.

THEY BELONGED TO GOD'S FAMILY

Paul writes to those **who belong to God our Father** . . . When you are in danger of being thrown out of home or losing your job just for being a Christian, it is tremendously comforting to know that you belong to somebody. Right from the beginning this letter reminds the Thessalonians that there was someone to care for them and look after them. They might be like refugee children with labels around their necks but they were in no danger of getting lost or being forgotten. And though people around treated them like dirt, these new Christians knew that they were 'somebodies' in God's eyes. He had adopted them into his family. They belonged to him.

What confidence this gave them for the future. When God adopts people he does not then leave them as spiritual orphans. He never abandons his children, no matter how feeble or rebellious they turn out to be. Paul firmly believed this. We can read about it in another letter he wrote. There he is talking to his friends in Philippi and he says, 'And so I am sure that God, who began this good work in you, will carry it on until it is finished on the Day of Christ Jesus.' (Philippians 1:6) He is not like many do-it-yourself enthusiasts. He does not litter the place with unfinished jobs. Instead, he completes what he has begun.

God the Father is not just the Father of the Lord Jesus Christ. He is 'our' Father, writes Paul – which means that we belong to one another as well as to him. Paul, Silas and Timothy are backing the Thessalonians to the hilt because they are not just casual friends. They are brothers in Christ. It is quite clear from the rest of the New Testament that the church should see itself as one worldwide family. And its motto, like that of the Three Musketeers, should be 'All for one and one for all'.

Paul writes to those **who belong to . . . the Lord Jesus Christ.**

As the going gets tough, they are to remember that Jesus Christ has gone before them. He is the pioneer. God the Father sent him into the world. His mission was not accomplished without taking risks. He had to face angry crowds and mocking mobs. He knew what suffering was. If we belong to Jesus we too must be prepared to face the same kind of reaction. He has shown us the way to go about it. And the power which enabled Jesus to face his job is now working in the Thessalonians.

The mission of Jesus came to its climax in his death, and in his rising from the tomb. This shows clearly how God can win through. When everything seems lost, he can bring about an amazing turn of events.

The Christian needs to think like a secret service agent. The agent must obey his instructions to the letter. He must recognize that he does not always understand the reasons behind the orders he is given. He cannot tell how things will work out. He must be ready for unexpected developments. He must learn to live with unanswered questions, for the total picture has not been revealed to him. It is only at the end of the assignment that the whole thing may be explained.

So the Christian serves Jesus Christ who is *the Lord*. In personal terms that means being prepared to give him our total allegiance. And in a much wider sense it means realizing that the Lord Jesus Christ is master-minding the whole complex operation. He is working in many secret and surprising ways.

THEY WERE WELL SUPPLIED

On the face of it, it seemed unlikely that these young Christians would survive alone. Thessalonica was such a hostile place. They would need outside help – and they got it. From heaven! God sent them hidden supplies. **May God our Father and the Lord Jesus Christ give you grace and peace.** No one on earth could cut off this power supply. When Paul says grace and peace come from the Father and Jesus he does not mean there are two separate sources, like the hot and cold water taps. Rather, God the Father is the source and the Lord Jesus Christ is the channel. While Jesus lived here on earth his life was full of grace and peace. And he had to face far greater pressures than any of us. So he knows how and when to give us these gifts to help us cope with our problems.

Paul recognized that grace and peace come from God, but he also knew that the supply is not automatic. So (as we can see from the opening greetings in all of his letters) he made it a matter of regular prayer that nothing should clog the flow. Right now, this was just the prayer the Thessalonians needed most. They wanted grace to help them keep going and find forgiveness when they failed. They needed that peace of God, which still baffles the world, to keep them from getting flustered.

The introductions over, Paul plunges into the matters uppermost in his mind. As we glance through this letter we get the impression that a number of the Thessalonians were beginning to have doubts. They wondered whether they could cope. Their jitters were understandable and in no way unusual. They were like a learner driver who has just passed his test. He ventures out for the first time on his own. Around him is a mass of fast, weaving, hooting traffic. There is no qualified driver at his elbow to say what to do, or grab the wheel in an emergency! The only way to gain confidence is to get experience!

Paul's opening greeting provides the encouraging word and steadying hand the believers at Thessalonica needed to set them back on the road again.

The relief column

(1:3-12)

It's the climax of a western film. The really dramatic moment has arrived. The besieged survivors are hopelessly outnumbered. They are low on provisions and short of ammunition. They cannot hope to hold out for much longer. Then, the exhausted defenders hear a bugle call from behind the enemy lines. They look up and can hardly believe their eyes. The long-awaited relief column has arrived. Suddenly the tables are turned. The cavalry slices through the enemy. Swords flash. The siege is lifted. A few moments before, they were surrounded. Now they are set free. The armies which had pinned them down are in full retreat.

This is the kind of picture Paul wants to paint for the Thessalonians here. Their position is desperate. But relief is on the way.

The long-awaited relief column has arrived.

HE REJOICES OVER THEM (v. 3)

When you feel like a failure, a dose of praise is a wonderful
tonic. Paul takes this line. He rejoices over the Thessalonians.
For the moment he ignores all the difficult issues and problem people. He saves any corrections and criticisms for
later. Generally speaking, he feels, the situation is very
encouraging. So he begins by giving them a five-star rating.
Our brothers, we must thank God at all times for you. And
that 'must' does not suggest that Paul and his friends are in
any way reluctant. It's just the opposite. They couldn't have
stopped their 'thank yous' even if they'd tried. That's what
Paul means.

When an athlete does well, the audience bursts into ap-
plause. In the same way, Paul and his friends want to show
the Thessalonians how pleased they are. They simply cannot
contain themselves. They are bubbling over with excitement
and mopping their brows with relief. Paul can just picture

the Thessalonians reading his words of praise. He can see them going red with embarrassment. So he reassures them by explaining. **It is right for us to do so.**

And it's not just a brief pat on the back. Paul kept up his thanks and praise **at all times.** Some people are always praising others. They want to keep on their right side and so their words lose all meaning. They go on and on like a gramophone record when the needle is stuck in the groove. There is nothing mechanical about Paul's praise. He really means it.

But why was Paul so full of joy? He, himself, gives two reasons. He tells the Thessalonians that it is **because your faith is growing so much and the love each of you has for the other is becoming greater.** Paul has been praying for both these things. In his first letter he had told the Thessalonians, 'Day and night we ask him with all our heart to let us see you personally and supply what is needed in your *faith.*' And as he wrote he had prayed, 'May the Lord make your *love* for one another and for all people grow more and more and become as great as our love for you.' (See 1 Thessalonians 3:10, 12) Now it has happened. He is really thrilled. It is a dramatic answer to his prayers.

Paul had the courage to pray for definite things. Because of this he had no difficulty in recognizing the answers when they came. Vague and muddled prayers bring no such reward. They are like firing arrows into a fog. Even if you hit the target, you never know.

The church in Thessalonica was continuing to grow. The enemies of Christ were trying to kill the church. They were spreading evil like poison. But all this was having the opposite effect. It was acting as a fertilizer! The church was not withering away. Instead it was fairly shooting up and blossoming out. The faith of its members was deeply rooted and therefore it did not wilt under the hot sun of persecution. God himself supplied their love. It was strong and sweet-smelling. The weedkiller of hatred could not destroy it. Its perfume spread everywhere. It built up until it became overpowering.

Church growth is not just to be measured in terms of numbers. God wants quality as well as quantity. This is Paul's desire too. He is just as concerned to measure progress as to count heads.

HE BOASTS ABOUT THEM (v. 4)

The Thessalonians were certainly going through trying times. And their experiences were teaching them valuable lessons. These were things which could be passed on to other Christians. The groups of new believers springing up in and around Corinth needed to hear of these trials and triumphs. Yet the Thessalonians could not blow their own trumpets. It was for Paul and his co-workers to sing their praises. They were thrilled to do this. They knew it would help. **That is why we ourselves boast about you in the churches of God.** They spelled out the reasons too. **We boast about the way you continue to endure and believe through all the persecutions and sufferings you are experiencing.**

The Thessalonians were strong both in defence and attack. Their troubles had been many. Danger faced them on all sides, yet they had stood firm. No doubt the persecutions had left a trail of suffering: broken bodies, shattered nerves, lost jobs, and poverty. Christians must expect to cross swords with the devil. There'll certainly be casualties too. A spiritual battle may lead to spiritual scars. The Thessalonians found this out. Yet their spirits were not broken. The harder the enemy struck, the tougher the Thessalonians became. They learned a difficult lesson and put it into practice. After all they had found that the strongest form of defence was attack.

94

Paul had learned a lesson too. He now knew that groups of Christians could exist in the most impossible places. If the church could thrive in Thessalonica it could thrive anywhere. This was the encouraging news he passed on to other congregations. Today's church would profit by taking a leaf out of the apostle's book too. God really does bless his people in tough and unlikely situations. These facts need to be made known. It is enormously encouraging. They can really encourage others in similar circumstances and teach them important lessons.

We are not just looking for glowing success stories. We have to learn about the heartaches and costs which lie behind the headlines. We don't want the publicity man's glossy version. We need the full facts; then we will know how to react. Meanwhile we have to put up with the explanations of the cynics:

'Their leader is an exceptional man. Remove him and the whole thing will fizzle out.'

'Yes, but their crowds come from a wide area. They aren't local people. And most of their talent has been imported from outside.'

'Just look at their premises. They are modern, purpose-built. They aren't saddled like us with a Victorian barn of a place in a run-down area.'

'It's nice to hear about what happened over there, but it would never work here.'

HE ENCOURAGES THEM (vs. 5-10)

Now Paul comes out with a surprising statement. **All of this proves that God's judgement is just.** God lets the people suffer at the hands of their enemies. But he is with them. He does not want them to look on their troubles as a punishment but a prize! They have shown promise as new

95

recruits. Now God introduces them to a tough training programme to make them even more effective. He wants to turn them into front-line crack troops.

... and as a result you will become worthy of his Kingdom, for which you are suffering ...

Even when you are at your peak, you cannot pass the fitness test for heaven. The 'work out' prescribed by God for each of us is individually planned. It is designed to develop our spiritual muscles. When we begin to exercise muscles we didn't even know we had, it is a painful business. A Christian has to keep in training if his faith is to develop. And it's all in the best of causes! It's on behalf of the kingdom of heaven and to promote its progress in the world.

An athlete is chosen for the Olympic team beacause of his own efforts. However, **becoming worthy** of the kingdom is not like that. In the word he uses, Paul stresses the point that we are 'made worthy'. It is all of God's doing, not ours. When the factory inspector sticks the 'passed' label on a product, it is the manufacturer's guarantee, not the product's self-advertisement. It tells us that the article has been well made and thoroughly tested.

THE TABLES WILL BE TURNED (vs. 6, 7)

Paul has more words of encouragement for the Thessalonians. He shows them again that relief is on the way. Children are not the only ones who need telling things more than once. Adults too need encouraging again and again. In Thessalonica there were some who seemed to be in danger of letting things get on top of them. They felt like a pot-holer lost in a cave at the end of a maze of tunnels – trapped with no way out. Their flame of hope was beginning to flicker. Paul fanned it back to life throughout the first letter. And it's like that for Christians today. Their torch of hope may grow dim but it never goes out. They carry on because they know there is light at the end of the tunnel.

One day the tables will be turned. **God will do what is right; he will bring suffering on those who make you suffer, and he will give relief to you who suffer.** God does not punish because he is vicious but because he is just. Sometimes we seem to stress the love and mercy of God too much and then lose sight of his justice. Evil-doers fool themselves if they think that God is easy-going. They may imagine that they can do just what they like and escape scot-free, but whatever they sow they will one day reap. This is as much Jesus's teaching as Paul's.

Paul adds an afterthought. 'He will give relief to you who suffer, *and to us as well.*' This shows that the Thessalonians were not fighting a lone battle. It was no local flare-up but part of a wider pattern of violence.

And Paul needed God's relief in his part of the battlefield just as much as they did in theirs.

THE DISOBEDIENT WILL BE PUNISHED (vs. 7-9)

He will do this when the Lord Jesus appears from heaven with his mighty angels, with a flaming fire. On the surface it may seem that the enemy has it all his own way. However, the reality is just the opposite. He must not judge from outward appearances. All the time the armies of heaven are at hand. They may be well camouflaged now, but at a given moment they will come out into the open. The all-powerful, conquering Lord will appear, accompanied by his mighty agents. He will come in judgement **to punish those who reject God and who do not obey the Good News about our Lord Jesus.**

Among the church's opponents at Thessalonica were many to whom God was about as real as Father Christmas. Others, mainly Jews, talked a lot about him but didn't know him in a deep personal way. They had turned their backs on his rescue plans. Yet both groups in Thessalonica had seen clear evidence of God's presence in the lives of Paul and his friends. They noticed the difference – yet even so they did not bother to ask the reason why. They chose to close their minds to the evidence. They were just like the man walking along a jungle trail. He rounds a bend to find a snarling tiger in his path. So he closes his eyes and puts his fingers in his

'Read all about it!'

ears. He simply pretends it is not really there. He even hopes that when he opens his eyes and takes his fingers out of his ears it will have gone away. These people have decided not to believe the message. They refuse to do anything about it. In Paul's words, they did **not obey the Good News about our Lord Jesus.**

What was this Good News? Paul is fond of shouting out the headlines loud and clear. 'Read all about it.'

GOD'S SON ON RESCUE MISSION

JESUS LAYS DOWN LIFE FOR THE GUILTY

FREE PARDON FOR CONDEMNED MEN

BELIEVE IN HIM AND RECEIVE HIS SPIRIT

IT'S THE ONLY WAY

FULL FACTS HERE

READ ALL ABOUT IT!

Paul was handling hot news. He wanted people to get the message about Jesus. He was glad that many did. But others just tore up their copies of the Good News. They rejected Jesus and his free pardon. What will happen to them?

They will suffer the punishment of eternal destruction, separated from the presence of the Lord and from his glorious might. Paul spells out the dreadful nature of the punishment. It will not be over quickly. It is eternal destruction. When murderers were executed it was fast and final. But God's punishment is different. *Eternal* means without end. The key thought here is not extermination but separation. They will be cut off from the presence of the Lord.

Separation does not simply mean that unbelievers will be left to their own devices. It will not be like school children enjoying themselves because teacher is out of the room. Nor will it be like a teenage party when the parents go away for the week-end and leave the youngsters on their own. Instead, it will mean that they are completely alone. Then for the first time in their lives they will miss God. They will no longer enjoy anything that is good or beautiful. Everything like that comes from God and now the supplies will be stopped. And what a state they'll be in. They will be in the clutches of hate, loneliness and misery – and all because they are separated from God's **glorious might**. His power has stopped the world getting out of hand and given it law and order. His glory has helped men to see the difference between right and wrong, between beauty and ugliness. And now it is too late to appreciate it.

The terrible situation which results will be all man's fault, not God's.

THE BELIEVERS WILL RECEIVE THE LORD WITH REJOICING (v. 10)

Punishment is only one side of the coin. Paul quickly flips it over to show the other side. He is no grim-faced prophet of doom. The weight of his message is not gloom but glory. There are celebrations ahead but God's mighty acts of judgement are needed to prepare the way. **When he comes on that Day to receive glory from all his people and honour from all who believe.** 'That Day' is not a tomorrow which never comes. Although here on earth we do not know the date of Jesus's coming, it is clearly marked on heaven's calendar.

The joy of that day will outshine anything we have felt before. It will be far beyond our wildest dreams.

When soldiers return home after a long tour of duty, it's an emotional time. At stations and airports the relatives wait excitedly. For months, wives, fiancées, parents and children have lived for that first glimpse of the one they love. They have carefully rehearsed their first words. Then the actual moment arrives and they rush into each other's arms. It is too marvellous for words. The only way they can express themselves is in tears, hugs and laughter.

And Paul reassures us, as well as the Thessalonians. **You too will be among them, because you have believed the message that we told you.** We saw from Paul's first letter that no one will miss out. Even those who may die before this great moment, will share in it. Nearly 2000 years have passed since the ink dried on this letter, yet its promise still holds true. We do not receive an entrance ticket to the celebrations for good behaviour. We are allowed in for 'believing the message'. We must put our whole trust in Christ. It is he who saves us.

HE PRAYS FOR THEM (vs. 11, 12)

God had willing servants in Thessalonica who were ready for anything. He is right behind them and will not let them down. He has promised them his loving care and shown them his goodness. Many people take their salvation for granted. They have a 'now, I'm all right Jack' attitude. Paul points out that they must become worthy of their new life. They must want to grow and the only way they can do this is if God helps them. **That is why we always pray for you. We ask our God to make you worthy of the life he has called for you to live.** God gives the means but we must put them to good use. If we want to gain anything, we must work for it. There are two ways of reaching the top of an oak tree. You can either climb one, or sit on an acorn and wait for it to grow! Our desire for goodness must be matched by our work of faith. Only then will we feel God's power. So Paul prays,

May he fulfil by his power all your desire for goodness and complete your work of faith. God does not disappoint us. He does not leave us with shattered ideals and projects in ruins. Whatever God does he does well.

Why is it so important for the church to show clear evidence of goodness and faith? One reason is to make a real impact on the world. But Paul has an even more important reason up his sleeve. **In this way the name of our Lord Jesus will receive glory from you . . .** Glory describes the blinding brightness of God's presence. It is not surface shine, but inner sparkle.

There are two ways of reaching the top of an oak tree.

A first-class product carries the maker's name. This guarantees its quality and the skills of the manufacturer. The Christian should be proud to wear the label 'Jesus Christ'. It shows who has shaped his life. When the quality is clear and the label is noticed, Jesus gets the glory.

How do we come to possess 'glory' to beam to the Lord? Paul tells us in his second letter to the Christians in Corinth. God has given it to us by his Spirit. 'That same glory, coming from the Lord, who is the Spirit, transforms us into his likeness in an ever greater degree of glory.' (2 Corinthians 3:18) God receives glory when the character of Jesus is seen in his followers. Our Lord will receive glory from you, **and you from him, by the grace of our God and of the Lord Jesus Christ**. At night it is the moon which lights the sky but it could not do this alone. The light it gives comes from the sun. The moon simply reflects it. In the same way, we can only see God's glory when it is reflected in the lives of his people. But on the last day the source will appear in person. Then dazzling glory will flood the earth.

Any time now?

(2:1, 2, 5)

'Perhaps he came while I was out?'

'Maybe I didn't hear the doorbell for the noise of the television.'

Have you ever waited for a friend to come? If so, you will probably have had thoughts like these rushing through your head. It is even worse when the friend is coming from overseas. You haven't seen him for years. You know he is due home any time, but you haven't been told the exact day. His flight number hasn't been confirmed so you cannot go to meet him. You simply wait until he turns up on the doorstep. And it is this waiting that starts the anxious questioning.

'Maybe he has been held up.'

'Perhaps he is not coming. After all, it is some years now since we last saw him. He may not feel the same way about us any more.'

As we saw in Paul's first letter, there were some Christians in Thessalonica who were expecting the Lord Jesus to return to earth from heaven at any moment. There was nothing odd about this belief. Before Christ left this earth he made it crystal clear that he hadn't disappeared for good. His ticket to heaven was a return, not one way. And Christians were to keep on their toes, he said. They must be alert and ready for his return. However this had caused problems with one group in Thessalonica. They wanted Jesus to return so much. You would think that this would have prodded them into action, but no! It had just the opposite effect. Instead of preparing for the great day, they became sky-watchers. It was as if they were paralysed.

And this wasn't all. In their excitement, they had begun to spread wrong ideas around. They had not paid any attention to Paul's warning in his first letter. So he returns once more to the subject. **Concerning the coming of our Lord Jesus Christ and our being gathered together to be with him: I beg you, my brothers, not to be so easily confused in your thinking or upset by the claim that the Day of the Lord has come.** Their thoughts were in a tangle. So Paul had some unravelling to do.

Paul hammers his point home. The Lord will come suddenly. There will be no announcement. He had told them this when he was with them. He had even confirmed it in writing. Now he says it again. 'Jesus will come out of the blue. So don't waste your time building an early-warning system. Don't leave everything till the last minute. Be alert at all times.'

At least the Thessalonians were clear about two things. There was no doubt in their minds that the Lord was returning. And they knew that they would then go to be with him. He would gather together all his people. However in their eagerness and excitement they had misunderstood one important point. When Paul said the Lord would come 'suddenly', they thought he meant 'immediately'. This prospect set them all of a dither. The ground rocked beneath their feet and they panicked. They became so worked up they could no longer think straight. Paul could not get through to them.

The Thessalonians really went off at the deep end, and so have many others after them. Throughout the ages Bible students have been predicting the exact moment of the Lord's return. They calculate with care the time of his coming and gather a group of excited followers. When the great day dawns, they climb a mountain and wait for Jesus to appear. Then, when he fails to show up, they reshuffle the figures to produce a different answer. That's not the way to prepare for Jesus to come. It's not by arguing over arithmetic. No prize is awarded for guessing the date.

The Bible contains lots of references to the last days. They are scattered about like pieces in a jigsaw puzzle. But when we try to put them together, we find that some of the pieces are missing. This adds to our confusion. And the temptation is strong to force in all the bits we can find, even if they make up the wrong picture.

When we come face to face with uncertainties, the arguments begin and doubts arise. The Thessalonians felt very mixed up about the day of the Lord's coming. Some of them could think of nothing else. The idea of his speedy return gripped them. They were sure they could see signs of his arrival everywhere. Others actually claimed that he had already come.

It was rather like France in 1944. The people in Normandy did not know the date of D-day. They had to live with rumours and false alarms. They listened to the coded messages broadcast from London to the French Resistance. Although they did not understand what they meant, it all sounded promising. Reconnaissance planes were spotted overhead. There was news of regular heavy bombing raids. There were tales of parachute drops and commando hit-and-run attacks. On many a morning people got up saying hopefully to themselves, 'This is the day.' But as soon as the off-shore naval bombardment began and the beach-head landings took place, everyone knew D-day had arrived. The actual occupation put an end to the arguments once and for all.

In New Testament times the Christian church was passing round coded messages about the Lord's return. The Thessalonians added their own interpretation. They wondered and they worried. Some were beginning to believe the false stories that Christ was back already. So Paul steps in to calm them down and squash the rumours. He brings them down to earth when he reminds them that a great deal has still to happen before the Lord returns.

How had this false teaching arisen? While he was in Thessalonica Paul had spoken to different groups in a variety of places. It was only natural that once he left, the young church should set about piecing together his teaching on a number of topics. Then the arguments started. What had Paul really said about Christ's return to earth? In an attempt to put two and two together, they made five!

Paul tries to jog their memory. He wants to know where he had been misunderstood and wrongly reported. **Perhaps it is thought that we said this while prophesying.** In the New Testament church the service didn't always run to a set pattern. One sermon might be advertised but sometimes two or more were preached. People were often inspired to give a brief, unprepared talk. When such a message came directly from the Lord it was called prophecy. Paul himself sometimes spoke in this way, and some over-enthusiastic believer may have misquoted him. There would be nothing unusual about that.

But it might not have been a prophecy. Someone may have misunderstood his *preaching*. Rumours can grow in many ways. Paul was not a one-sermon-a-week man. He never lost an opportunity to proclaim the gospel to unbelievers. And he was just as keen to teach new Christians fresh truths about their faith. He had left them with many hours of instruction to remember, and none of it was recorded on tape.

There was a third possibility. Paul says ... **or that we wrote it in a letter.** Groups of Christians were scattered all over Greece. It was a great day when they received a letter, especially one from Paul. And it can be so easy to misread things when we are excited. This could easily have happened in Thessalonica.

But Paul might have been thinking of something more sinister. He had many enemies who did not agree with his teaching. They might want to discredit him amongst his friends. Perhaps someone had forged a letter in his name.

It might even have been another Christian who had written the letter. Paul's friendship meant importance. A letter from him would make your friends take notice.

As time went on, more and more phoney letters and stories of Christ appeared. This caused people to become confused. They were not sure which were genuine and which were fakes. They even began to ask questions about the real truths of the Christian message. Church leaders realized that something had to be done. So they drew up a list of letters and other documents which were known to be genuine and which told the truth about Jesus. Today, we call this collection the New Testament. But in Paul's day, things were not so well organized. He and the other apostles had to keep their eyes open and their ears to the ground. They had to make sure that all the teaching passed on in their name was true.

THEY WERE FORGETFUL

Paul is like a despairing schoolmaster. The Thessalonians had really made a mess of their homework. **Don't you remember?** he asks. 'Even the basic facts about the Lord's coming? I told you about it often enough. You can't say "You never told us".'

Yet still they couldn't get it right. Important truths bear repetition. A good teacher goes over the same ground again and again. And to avoid this becoming boring Paul approaches the subject in different ways. Jesus himself taught important lessons many times until the penny dropped. And even then his hearers needed their memories jogged from time to time.

Before moving on to the next section, we must face up to a difficulty. None of us was in Thessalonica when Paul taught about the Lord's coming. This causes problems. When Paul asks, **Don't you remember? I told you all this while I was with you,** we have to reply, 'No I don't remember. I wasn't there!' All we have to go on is the brief outline in the letter. The

Thessalonians could fill in the rest from memory. We cannot.

We have another problem too. Paul is not writing openly on the subject. He is being deliberately secretive. The letter might fall into the wrong hands. It might be taken by the Roman authorities and used in evidence against the church. Therefore when Paul talked about the heads of state, he had to hide his teaching in vague language. Otherwise he could easily land himself and the church in serious trouble. So this part of the letter contains hints which are lost on us. After all, Paul did not intend *us* to read his words, any more than the Emperor at Rome.

We go on to tackle this very puzzling section of Paul's letter in the next chapter. It is difficult and the best that we can do is to offer suggestions. Perhaps Peter had this passage in mind when he wrote about Paul, 'There are some difficult things in his letters which ignorant and unstable people explain falsely'. (2 Peter 3:16) Many Bible experts describe chapter two of this letter as the most difficult in the New Testament. So you will need to wear your thinking cap and have an ice-pack at the ready as we move on!

The masked outlaw

(2:3-12)

The last outlaw did not disappear with the taming of America's Wild West Frontier. This section of Paul's letter tells us about an outlaw still to come. He will be far worse and have much greater power than any who have gone before him. He is here described as **the Wicked One.** We could also call him the Man of Lawlessness. He is a mysterious character. At the present time, he is 'masked' to keep his identity secret. He is difficult to track down. He is forced into using hit-and-run tactics, because circumstances prevent him from coming out into the open. But Paul reminds the Thessalonians that one day he will take off his mask and operate openly.

Paul is writing about terrible events still in the future. He wanted to correct the false idea that the Lord's coming was just round the corner. The Thessalonian Christians were mixed up enough about that already. So Paul takes them quickly through the points he has previously gone over in some detail.

THE OUTLAW WILL APPEAR (v. 3)

Do not let anyone deceive you in any way. For the Day will not come until the final Rebellion takes place and the Wicked One appears. Paul's readers must not be taken in. They are simply fooling themselves if they think that the future will be all rosy. Before the day of Jesus's return dawns, there will be a long, dark night. Then 'all hell' will be let loose. The church will have to muster all its strength if it is to withstand the explosion of evil. The Thessalonians were so excited that they had forgotten all about this darker side to Paul's teaching. They were prepared for the coming of Jesus, but not for any long delay in his arrival.

More than once the New Testament looks ahead to the end of the world. Moral and spiritual issues will become sharper. The pace will hot up.

People will be forced to declare their colours and stand their ground. It will not be possible to sit on the fence any longer. Everyone will have to come down one side or the other. Surrender to Christ and be safe! Reject him and expose yourself to his judgement and everlasting punishment! These are the only alternatives.

Tragically many will make the wrong choice. Every day people hear the gospel and enjoy the fringe benefits – yet still jump the wrong way.

Paul is not the only one to write about a great rebellion. We find the idea in Jesus's own teaching. He warned his followers that a stormy passage lay ahead of them. 'Then you will be arrested and handed over to be punished and be put to death. All mankind will hate you because of me. Many will give up their faith at that time; they will betray one another and hate one another. Then many false prophets will appear and deceive many people. Such will be the spread of evil that many people's love will grow cold. But whoever holds out to the end will be saved.' (Matthew 24:9-13) What will Christ's camp-followers do when they find the whole world set against them? Will they decide the moment has come to change sides? Perhaps – but genuine believers are not to be unduly alarmed. The Lord has promised them that they are secure in his hands. 'I give them eternal life, and they shall never die. No one can snatch them away from me.' (John 10:28) There is no danger of being kidnapped by the Enemy. The Lord provides foolproof security cover in the hottest battle.

In the past there have been lots of isolated revolts against God. People have protested against him, his standards and his Son. It has always been so. But here Paul has something far bigger in mind. It is the final great rebellion. There will be a worldwide, anti-God movement, he says, which will spread evil like a plague. And within this movement a man will suddenly appear who will make a take-over bid for world power.

Today, advertising men can be very cunning. They know how to promote an individual through television and the press. Within hours he can rocket from obscurity to stardom. If our age knows a lot about publicity, so does the Wicked

111

One. He will find no difficulty in putting over his image. He has popular appeal already and supernatural dramatic powers, with no need for script writers or make-up teams. His propaganda machine will condition men into believing and following him. His forces will cause chaos. They will tear society apart and create a power vacuum. He will then step in and seize control. It will be as easy as that.

So the Wicked One takes the scene. He is the devil's rival to Christ the Son of God (which is why he is described as 'Antichrist' elsewhere in Scripture). Like Jesus, he will 'appear' at the end of time. He too will come with power – but not God's. He will perform all kinds of miracles, signs and wonders, just as Christ did in his earthly ministry. But all the outlaw's 'Christian' works will really be clever forgeries. And men will have to inspect them very carefully to detect that they are fakes.

Antichrist is such a powerful enemy, and we will have to face him. No wonder we tremble! Paul knows how his readers feel, so quickly he adds that the Wicked One **is destined to hell.** Outlaws usually come to a sticky end, and this one is no exception. His fate is sealed, even before he shows up.

THE OUTLAW WILL DEMAND TO BE WORSHIPPED (v. 4)

When the Wicked One appears he will demand that everyone obeys him in everything – or else! He will let no one else be master, either here on earth or in heaven. **He will oppose every so-called god or object of worship.**

In Paul's day the Emperor in Rome stood for absolute power. His word was law. He demanded to be called Lord to show who was the boss. He even forced the people to treat him like a god. They had to make sacrifices to him. But the Christians stood firm against such blasphemy. They refused to worship the Emperor or even to call him 'Lord'. For them Christ alone was Lord. So they faced harsh penalties. Some were imprisoned and many were killed.

Paul warns his readers. The Wicked One will take things even further than the Roman Emperors. They were content to be gods together. But he must be the one and only god in the universe. **He will put himself above them all. He will even go in and sit down in God's temple and claim to be God.**

Paul was born a Jew. His background played an important part in his life. It shows through here in his warnings about the Wicked One. He wants to get a difficult point across, so in looking for illustrations which his Jewish readers will grasp, he refers back to two events in their national history.

In the second century BC a heathen king named Antiochus Epiphanes ransacked the temple at Jerusalem. He didn't think much of Israel's God and set up the image of his own god, Zeus, on the altar in the most holy place.

In AD 40 the Roman Emperor Caligula went further. He tried to set up a statue of himself in the same holy place. Only one thing stopped him in his tracks – sudden death.

Paul says the Wicked One will make Caligula look like a saint! He will attempt to take God's place – and not just in the Jerusalem temple. He will do more than set up a statue – he will seek to establish his throne. Not even the rank of archbishop will do for him – he has to be Almighty God. In modern political terms he will make himself a divine dictator in a police state. He will demand not only outward obedience but devoted worship.

Perhaps if Paul had been alive today he would have used the language of brain-washing. In China the old religions have been given up as outdated nonsense. Millions clutch their little Red Books instead of Bibles, and chant the thoughts of Chairman Mao like hymns. When people are deprived of religion, they quickly find God-substitutes.

THE OUTLAW IS RESTRICTED AT PRESENT
(vs. 6, 7)

Paul has been looking into the future when there will be open rebellion and the Wicked One will go on the rampage.

Now he brings us back to the present – to show us the outlaw already hard at work. We don't always realize it, because the Wicked One hides his identity by using many different disguises. His methods are like those of the modern urban guerrilla leader. He relies on hit-and-run tactics. After all, he is operating in the face of well-armed security forces. He cannot afford to come out into the open as long as he needs to gain popular sympathy for his cause. He keeps his own identity secret and uses middlemen. It's going to be a long job. So he has to be patient if he wants to win through in the end.

Yet there is something else that hinders the Wicked One. He cannot come right out into the open even if he wants to. In Paul's words, **there is something that keeps this from happening now, and you know what it is ... The Mysterious Wickedness is already at work, but what is going to happen will not happen until the one who holds it back is taken out of the way.** We don't have all the facts, so we can only guess at what Paul means here. What is the *something* which acts as a brake on the Wicked One? Who is the one who *holds back* the Mysterious Wickedness?

Over the years many people have tried to answer those questions. Most think that Paul is talking about law and order. Paul does not hesitate to call on Christians to obey the civil authorities, which in his day meant the Roman Empire. Rome gave the ancient world great principles of law and justice and protected civilization from chaos and anarchy. Even today, its laws are remembered and, in some countries, respected!

But this explanation does not solve all our problems.

Paul is talking not just about a principle but a person. He speaks of *someone* who holds back the Mysterious Wickedness. Who is this person? Many solutions have been suggested. Paul may mean the angel Michael, mentioned in the Old Testament book of Daniel and in Revelation in the New Testament. As we have seen, angels are God's agents. They carry out his orders. Michael's particular task is to restrain the Wicked One. This fits in with the job description which we read here. He is like a strong man who tries to dam a weakened river bank. He holds the sandbags in place to stop the river from bursting through in full flood.

THE OUTLAW WILL BE DESTROYED (v. 8)

The *Mysterious Wickedness* is already at work. It is 'mysterious' because its source is so hard to detect. There's certainly evil in the world. No one would argue with that. But where does it come from? Paul tells us that it comes from a person. One day, everyone will see it clearly for what it is – or, rather, see him for *who* he is! When the Wicked One thinks the time is right, he will drop his disguises and appear in person.

Then the Wicked One will be revealed. He is watching events with the eyes of a hungry tiger. He is ready to pounce. He is waiting for the right moment to gain control. But his victory won't last for long. Paul immediately adds, **but when the Lord Jesus comes, he will kill him with the breath from his mouth and destroy him with his dazzling presence.** As soon as the Wicked One has crashed on to the scene, the Lord himself will appear to turn the tables.

The resulting conflict will be short and sharp. In spite of the Wicked One's hideous strength, the Lord will deal with him easily and quickly. He will kill him with the breath from his mouth. He will not even have to dirty his hands. That will

115

be enough to put him out of action for good. 'Breath' is another way of saying 'word'. The Lord's word is all-powerful. It silenced the demons, stilled the storm and raised the dead. So, in the end, his word will exterminate the Wicked One as easily as a puff of breath snuffs out a candle.

THE OUTLAW WILL WORK WONDERS
(vs. 9, 10)

Although the Wicked One's fate is sealed, Paul does not want his readers to underestimate their enemy. He is very sly, as well as immensely arrogant. He is the master of disguise too – even able to appear as an angel of light. **The Wicked One will come with the power of Satan and perform all kinds of false miracles and wonders, and use every kind of wicked deceit on those who will perish.**

There is a warning to us here. Everywhere, people claim to have supernatural powers. Some say they can read minds. Others that they can foretell the future. Some even perform wonders on physical objects. They can move things without touching them. They can bend hard metal without the touch of a finger. Without doubt some who claim supernatural knowledge are 'cranks', and many so-called wonder-workers are frauds. Yet, we cannot explain everything away. Some startling performances are signs of the devil's power. But Paul warns us against getting involved. We can so easily become curious and begin to dabble. Many who start off 'just for fun' by reading tea-leaves or playing with an ouija board find out too late that they have been trapped by a sinister power from which there's no escape.

Dabbling in the supernatural is on the increase, and it attracts a great deal of publicity. In August 1975 the first ever world congress on Witchcraft took place in Bogota, South America. 3000 witches, sorcerers and spiritists

116

gathered in Colombia's capital. The programme advertised contact with the spirits of famous people from the past, including the Roman Emperor Nero, Hitler and Peron. It offered demonstrations of supernatural healing and painless invisible operations. Such events make us wonder what the Wicked One will get up to when he actually arrives on the scene!

THE OUTLAW WILL FIND A FOLLOWING
(vs. 10-12)

When people deliberately turn their back on the gospel of Christ they turn out the light. They may find it more fun to grope around in the dark. But if you do not have a light you cannot tell the difference between true and false. That's how the Wicked One will exploit the darkness in men's minds. He will deceive people with his false miracles and many will be fooled into following him. Too late they will discover that they have been conned. They had hoped to gain power with him. Instead they will be condemned to perish with him.

But it's not all the Wicked One's fault. His victims made the wrong decision long before he deceived them. They can't shift all the blame on to him. **They will perish because they did not welcome and love the truth so as to be saved. And so God sends the power of error to work in them so that they believe what is false.**

Christ has shown us the truth and explained it to us. What will happen if we refuse to believe him? His death means that we can be forgiven. But what if we turn our backs on him? He rose from the dead. But what if we ignore the evidence? Paul supplies the answers. God will allow our judgement, he says, to become warped and unreliable.

So many today reject the hard evidence of Christ in the

117

gospels. Instead they are ready to believe weird and wonderful tales about the meaning of life which in their right minds they would reject as ridiculous. In blunt language, Paul tells us that when we turn to false teaching, God will turn from us. He will blind us to reality. We will no longer be able to tell the difference between right and wrong. If we deliberately choose lies, we will be misled. If we are foolish enough to play with a lion, we will find ourselves in its den as food for the cubs. Once error is allowed out of the cage it cannot be controlled.

The result is that all who have not believed the truth, but have taken pleasure in sin, will be condemned. People like this have sold their souls to the Wicked One. They must therefore share his fate. God will condemn them.

We are now at the end of this most difficult section of Paul's letter. One further question remains. Who is the Wicked One?

Many people during the course of history have thought they could put a name to him. Some early Christians probably thought he was Nero. Other Roman Emperors who persecuted Christians also became strong candidates. At the time of the Reformation, the Protestants were sure it was the Pope. During the Second World War people put forward Hitler's name; in the Soviet Union, the persecuted believers thought Stalin fitted the role of the Wicked One perfectly. In the pressures of the moment, it is easy to make mistakes. All these men have come and gone, but the End is not yet. The Outlaw has still to appear – and he continues to wear his mask. But for how much longer?

Back to basics

(2:13-17)

In the last chapter we were flying high in thick storm clouds. Here we come nearer ground level and find ourselves back in the sunshine. Once again we enjoy improved visibility. It's a great relief to know where we are! From now on, until the end of the letter, the going is clear and straightforward.

Paul is not just a high-flying sky pilot. He earths all his teaching in the world of everyday life. In each of his letters he includes a practical section on Christian living. His letter to the Thessalonians is no exception. Having dealt with the complicated questions about Christ's return and the Wicked One, he gets back to the basics. He reminds his readers of all that the Lord has done for them. He is all too aware that as soon as Christians begin to take their salvation for granted they are in for trouble.

Some clever mathematicians are weak on their multiplication tables. They may even struggle with simple arithmetic. Yet this does not seem to stop them doing complicated calculations. But for the Christian it is altogether different. He must first grasp the ABC of God's Good News. If he fails here he will be wrong all along the line. He will be like a careless navigator on an intercontinental jet. His plane may start only a few degrees off its bearing. But by the time it should be reaching its destination it will be several hundred miles off course.

For the Christian there is nothing boring in going back to the basics. Even the 'simple' ABC of the gospel is a great wonder. Its message is packed so full of truth that there are always fresh things to discover. It is not like a multiplication table or the alphabet, which can be learned parrot-fashion and recited without thinking. On the one hand, it is so clear

119

They were like storm-battered ships returning to harbour.

that a child can understand. On the other, it is so deep that the world's greatest thinkers cannot touch bottom.

No, we don't know it all and we never can. There is still a lot to learn. So we happily go back to school for a refresher course. We may then be surprised at just how much we have forgotten or failed to put into practice!

Lesson One: THE LORD LOVES YOU (v. 13)

Paul now introduces some warmth and light. That last section of his teaching seemed so cold and gloomy! We **must** thank God at all times for you, brothers, you whom the Lord loves. Paul knew that the Thessalonians had taken a beating. They were like storm-battered ships returning to harbour. They were like wounded soldiers stumbling into the first-aid post. So he wanted his letter to give practical help. These Christian soldiers needed to be bandaged up, given new heart and kitted out for the battle that lay ahead.

When we feel cut-off and exhausted, we are tempted to think that nobody cares. We torture ourselves with questions. Why should this be happening to me? Why doesn't God step in to end this suffering? Has he turned his back on me? The Thessalonians were no different. So, to get rid of their doubts Paul calls them **you whom the Lord loves**. They have not been dumped on a spiritual junk-heap. God is right with them in the thick of all their battles. And his name is still Love.

If God has not abandoned them, neither has Paul. Once again he reminds them that he is always thinking about them and rejoicing over them. He has not taken them out of his memory file. Rather, he has kept them in his 'for action' tray. This gives him something to rejoice over each time he goes to God with his pile of problems!

That's the first lesson for Christians in trouble. They should be anchored to the fact that God loves them. It will help them ride out any storm. They will still get battered, but they will not become bitter. The Thessalonians had known all about this from the start. Paul began his first letter by reminding them, 'even though you suffered much, you received the message with the joy that comes from the Holy Spirit'. (1 Thessalonians 1:6)

Lesson Two: THE LORD HAS CHOSEN YOU (v. 13)

For God chose you as the first to be saved by the Spirit's

power to make you his holy people . . . The Christians to whom Paul was writing were only the first batch of believers at Thessalonica. They were not the full consignment but just a small sample to show what was possible on a much larger scale. They were like the new models at the motor show, on display to persuade the public to buy. The Thessalonian Christians knew that they were very ordinary people. Yet the Lord had been able to use them. He had done wonderful things with them. From 'two stroke' power the Lord had given them a high-performance potential. And because they were not very special people, they were splendid advertisements. If God could do it for them he could do it for anyone!

We cannot make people into Christians. Only God can do that, for it needs nothing less than a miracle. And it's a good job the choice is his. If we did the picking and choosing we might just go to 'nice' people. We would look for our kind of folk. But we know that it does not happen that way. Because God is in control, it is sometimes the most unlikely people who turn to him. Paul himself was a good example. He persecuted Christians. Yet God did not reject him. Instead he was specially picked out to be a pioneer missionary. This surprising turn-about bowled the church right over. For weeks afterwards they were scratching their heads in sheer disbelief. Could God really choose a man like that? He wouldn't have made their short-list.

If we then go on to ask, '*When* does God do the choosing?' we are in for a big surprise. Instead of the words, 'For God chose you *as the first* to be saved', Paul may have meant 'For God chose you *from the beginning* to be saved'. We can't be absolutely certain which he wrote. But whichever it was, the idea of God choosing us 'from the beginning' is a theme we often find in his letters. He does not mean the moment when we first heard the message and said 'yes' to it. Or even our date of birth. We have to look at his letter to the Christians in Ephesus to see what he really means. Then

122

we find he pushes the beginning right back beyond the horizons of time. 'Even before the world was made, God had already chosen us to be his, through our union with Christ . . .' (Ephesians 1:4) God chose us long ago, way back beyond the time when we were just twinkles in grandfather's eye – before there even was a grandfather.

And it's all God's doing. The Thessalonians are what they are because of him. He has chosen them. His Spirit has given them new life and power. Just the tonic they needed! It was not merely that they had placed their hand in his; his arms were under them – it was that way round. There are times when we find ourselves in a tight spot or doubt our ability to hang on to God. We may be afraid that our grip will fail. Then we need to remember that it is he who holds us safe. And he will not let us slip through his fingers.

Lesson Three: THE LORD HAS CALLED YOU
(v. 14)

God called you to this through the Good News we preached to you; he called you to possess your share of the glory of our Lord Jesus Christ. Choosing comes before calling. When a national soccer team is picked, the selection board meets to draw up a list of names. Then the players are contacted and called together. Although they have been selected, they know nothing about it until the call reaches them by letter or telephone. Only then do they know for sure that they are really in the team. Then is the time for celebration!

How were the Thessalonians called into the family of God? They didn't really need to be reminded. It was through the Good News that Paul had preached to them. Paul and his friends had delivered an invitation from God with an RSVP attached. Their hearers knew that the message did not come from the apostles. It was from God himself.

123

And when they accepted it God's Holy Spirit filled their lives. They knew that without any shadow of a doubt. Now they were quite sure they were God's children. And the end result was that they had become share-holders in the Lord's glory.

God's call is for a purpose, **to possess your share of the glory of our Lord Jesus Christ.** God is not like a generous prospector. He does not invite us to share in a gold rush and grab what we can. He is more like a solicitor who calls us into his office to receive an inheritance. The cheque is ours. It is made out in our name. If we refuse to cash it, we will miss out on our share of the glory. But in that case we only have ourselves to blame for our spiritual poverty.

Glory is shorthand for all the dazzling qualities of Christ's life, which Christians can share through faith. And his life is a brilliantly clear picture of what God is like and what life is like in heaven. Even here on earth the church is meant to glow with that glory.

It is Sunday morning. There is a visitor in our church. He has never heard of Jesus Christ and has certainly never read the gospels. He can only learn about our Lord by watching us closely as individuals and as a group. He is trying to draw up a profile of this Jesus we worship. He is looking for God – the God we say lives in us and amongst us by his Spirit. How close will he get to Jesus's character and job-description? If we want people to take us seriously as Christians we will need more than clever arguments. We will have to show them, not just tell them. After all, Christ has shared his glory with us. So we must not pull down the blinds. We have to be faithful reflections of him in all that we do and claim to be. If not, we are guilty of breaking the spiritual Trades Descriptions Act. When glory is really seen in the church, it should be always more, not less, than advertised.

Lesson Four: STAND FIRM (v. 15)

God has done so much for us. But even this has its dangers. He does not want us to sit back and do nothing like guests in a five-star heavenly hotel. We have our part to play as well.

God has given us his Good News. So now it's up to us. We must place our faith in the truth. And that is not just high-sounding pulpit talk. It is something very practical. We all know the theory of the parachute. We've seen people jump, so we know how it works. However, the question remains, 'Are we prepared to jump out of an aircraft at 5000 feet before pulling the ripcord?' That's faith! And once the parachute has opened, we must trust it to land us safely. **So then, our brothers, stand firm and hold on to those truths which we taught you, both in our preaching and in our letter.**

Stand firm! The Thessalonians had been constantly under attack ever since they first hoisted the flag of Christ. They must have wanted so much to give up and get out. But their gospel fortress was strong enough to take all the enemy's fire. They must not give an inch. They were fighting their spiritual El Alamein.

Hold on! They must not slacken their grip on the gospel rope. They must not let the great truths which supported their faith slip through their fingers. So whatever the pressure the order of the day was – 'hang on'. After all, there's no safety net to catch those who fall.

Lesson Five: THE LORD WILL MAKE YOU STRONG (vs. 16, 17)

Paul's words here provide more than a morale booster for war-weary soldiers in Thessalonica. He has been urging them on. They must keep up their effort. But he knows that they will need more than their own resources to win through. Therefore, he reminds them that God has given them the strength they need. That is how they have managed so far. **. . . our Lord Jesus Christ himself and God our Father, who loved us and in his grace gave us unfailing courage and a firm hope.** Their bravery would not evaporate as the battle hotted up. It had survival quality because God was its source. And their hope was not the rash optimism of the gambler. It rested on the most certain of all safe bets – the sure promises of God.

Paul has been looking back at his readers' past experience. He has taught with examples, their own examples. Now he turns to the present. He prays for the Thessalonians as they are now. **May our Lord Jesus Christ himself, and God our Father . . . encourage you and strengthen you to always do and say what is good.** It took courage for the Thessalonians to speak out. They knew what was right and true and they had to show it by their words and actions. Christians living in pagan societies often find themselves fighting popular opinion. If we are to take a stand for Christ and face the consequences we need to be very sure of our own convictions. No one finds it easy to be the odd man out. But one plus God is always a majority.

On the hot-line

(3:1-5)

In a busy office the telephone is going all the time. The staff need to keep in close contact both with head office and with their many clients. In Paul's letters there are hints that he is under pressure as he writes. Sometimes his thoughts are a little disconnected. Perhaps he is worried by other things and annoyed by constant interruptions. And at the same time he is dictating his letters he is on the hot-line to heaven. Paul's letters are punctuated with prayers. One such prayer popped up at the end of the last section. His motto seems to have been 'When you pause, pray'.

Often he shares his memos from Head Office with his clients. This gives them added confidence in him. For they know he goes right to the top when he discusses their affairs.

Finally, our brothers . . . as we saw in the first letter, 'finally' does not mean that Paul is about to finish. Rather, it marks a breathing space. There was not a daily post from Corinth to Thessalonica. Each letter had to be carried by hand and reliable messengers were few and far between. Paul had to be sure his letter was exactly right. He could not afford to leave anything out. He might have to wait a long time for the next post if he wanted to add a PS!

So here he pauses. Perhaps he asked his secretary to read through what he had already written. Then he could see what he had missed out and needed to mention! And by pausing for breath he sometimes got second wind, which meant that he carried on longer than he intended!

YOU PRAY FOR US (vs. 1, 2)

In the Christian world it is not just senior management who can use the hot-line to the top. Every Christian and church has direct communication with the Lord. So Paul, as well as praying for his converts, asks them to pray for him. Praying is something we must learn to do for each other.

Finally, our brothers, pray for us . . . We learn something about Paul from that sentence. He shows us what a giant he was. He may have been a great leader, and he certainly had many natural abilities. Yet he was a humble man. He knew he needed God and was not afraid to admit it. God had given him great authority. When Paul spoke, people listened. But this did not cut him off from them. He puts himself on the same level as the newest converts in Thessalonica and asks for their prayers. He wants them to look after him in this way. He really believes that their prayers work just as well as his own, and can do wonders for him.

Paul has problems to face in Corinth. He therefore asks them to pray about two matters in particular.

1. For the message – that it may race on.
2. For the messengers – that they may be rescued.

From the wonderful results which followed it appears that the Thessalonians did as Paul asked. The story of his visit to Corinth is told in the book of Acts. There we can read of the incredible things that happened. All of it shows how God answers prayer.

PRAY THAT THE MESSAGE WILL RACE ON

. . . pray for us, that the Lord's message may continue to spread rapidly and be received with honour . . . The word which Paul actually uses for 'spread rapidly' is 'run'. He imagines God's word has legs. As he writes, he pictures the sports stadium with an athlete speeding down the track. He is thrilled at the pace, but nervous in case anything should go wrong! What if someone should get in the way? What if the runner stumbles and fades after such a brilliant sprint start?

Paul is not ashamed to work for rapid results. He looks at the world around him. It is so needy and the gospel message is so vital. He must not rest now. There were signs that many people were beginning to catch on to the good news he was

128

announcing. All the more reason, therefore, not to lose a single chance. An alert salesman redoubles his efforts in those areas where a market is opening up. However, Paul never went for quantity at the expense of quality. He wanted the Lord's message not only to 'spread rapidly', but also to be *received with honour* at the same time. Sheer quantity without quality is worthless.

Paul wants his converts to show that they are now living a new kind of life. They must become living advertisements for the power of the gospel, both as individuals and as a community. He hopes then that their neighbours will notice the change and that when they have examined the gospel they will want it for themselves.

He prays that the Christian message will run quickly and be received with honour. He pictures it receiving an Olympic gold medal for its sparkling performance. For God's message can do wonderful things. We give the message glory not simply for what it reveals and claims. We give it glory for what it does. It turns worthless lives into precious gold. If it can perform that kind of miracle it deserves a medal!

... **just as it was among you.** Paul recalls those unforgettable moments in Thessalonica when he first introduced the gospel to the people. It was like dropping a stone in a huge pond – the ripples spread hundreds of miles. As he wrote in his first letter, 'For not only did the message about the Lord go out from you throughout Macedonia and Achaia, but the news about your faith in God has gone everywhere.' (1 Thessalonians 1:8)

After Thessalonica, Paul had gone on to Berea. There he had further success. In fact the initial response was even greater than in Thessalonica. We can read about it in Luke's diary of Paul's travels. In his report on Berea he says, 'The people there were more open-minded than the people in Thessalonica. They listened to the message with great eagerness, and every day they studied the Scriptures to see if what

Paul said was really true. Many of them believed; and many Greek women of high social standing and many Greek men also believed.' (Acts 17:11, 12) If anything, the gospel had increased its pace on the Berea lap.

But when Paul got to Athens it was a different story. It is true that he managed to speak to the leading debaters in the city. He tried really hard to put over his message. He drew on the Athenians' background, working in familiar quotations from two of their poets. He thought that might make them prick up their ears. But they weren't in the mood to respond. In spite of all his efforts, he had very poor results. Again Luke picks up the story: 'Some men joined him and believed, among whom was Dionysius, a member of the Council; there was also a woman named Damaris, and some other people.' (Acts 17:34) On the whole, there was not very much to report.

Paul's next port of call was Corinth. That was the last place on earth he wanted to visit at a time when he was feeling really depressed! His confidence was shaken. His strength was drained. Rather than going into the ring for a good fight he felt like lying down for the count of ten. But there was no chance for a rest. Instead he had to take on Corinth, a city known the world over for its way-out ideas, its wild living and its seamy night life.

If his reception at Athens had been too cool, Paul found Corinth too warm for comfort. The synagogue congregation gave him a rough time. He reacted strongly. Luke reports, 'When they opposed him and said evil things about him, he protested by shaking the dust from his clothes and saying to them: "If you are lost, you yourself must take the blame for it! I am not responsible. From now on I will go to the Gentiles." So he left them and went to live in the house of a Gentile named Titius Justus, who worshipped God; his house was next to a synagogue.' (Acts 18:6-7) The fact that Paul had set up in opposition next door to their own headquarters made these Jews see red. It wasn't exactly a tactful move!

So there's Paul, sitting in Justus's house in Corinth. He isn't writing from a safe suburb. He is in a trouble spot. He is concerned that his ministry should not run out of steam at this difficult stage. So he sends off word to the Thessalonians. He asks for their help. Will they please pray for his work? He is eager that the Lord's message will spread quickly and gather glory, even there in Corinth. The Thessalonians did what Paul asked. They got through on the hot-line to heaven. And God answered their request far beyond their wildest dreams. Soon things began to happen in Corinth. God's word moved into top gear. Luke records the wonderful results: 'Crispus, who was the leader of the synagogue, believed in the Lord, together with all his family; and many other people in Corinth heard the message, believed, and were baptized.' (Acts 18:8)

Not only did God's message spread rapidly. In a spectacular way it won over the most unlikely people. The new converts were not all drawn from the respectable end of town. They included, in Paul's own words, those who had been immoral, idol worshippers, adulterers, homosexual perverts, thieves, greedy people, drunkards and slanderers. (1 Corinthians 6:9, 10) A mixed congregation if ever there was one!

That was their first prayer answered!

If ever the news got back to the Thessalonians they must have been stunned by God's startling performance. But there was more to come, as God set about answering the second prayer just as remarkably as the first.

Paul knows only too well that he and his team are in great danger at Corinth. Therefore he writes, **Pray also that God will rescue us from wicked and evil people.** Ever since the riots in Philippi, his Jewish enemies have been hot on the trail. They had succeeded in throwing the missionaries out of Thessalonica and Berea. Now they were stirring things up in Corinth. Matters finally came to a head when the Jews seized Paul and took him to court. A new Roman governor had recently been appointed. So the Jews were eager to see if he would dole out a stiff penalty for unlawful religious activities.

But the prayers of God's people provided special protection for Paul and his friends. The Jews presented their case badly. And Gallio, the governor, considered they were making a mountain out of a mole-hill. He refused to take any action. So Paul was allowed to keep on with his work in Corinth for many days more.

It had been a dangerous and difficult time. Paul and his friends must have suffered both mentally and physically. They must have had quite a story to tell. If they had lived today, there might well have been some new and exciting paperbacks on our shelves. *Crisis at Corinth* by Aquila, or *The Siege of the Synagogue* by Sosthenes, would make interesting reading. Yet Paul dismisses the whole story in a few words. He does not give any lurid details. There is no blow-by-blow description of the clash. Above all he does not try to make a martyr of himself. He tells the Thessalonians that he is in danger. He goes on simply, **For not everyone believes the message.** Then he cuts short the discussion of his own problems and switches attention back to the Lord he serves.

WE'LL PRAY FOR YOU (vs. 3-5)

Paul reminds the Thessalonians that the Lord will not let them down. And this gives his own memory a jog. **The Lord is faithful.** Though separated by hundreds of miles he and his readers were facing the same dangers. Like two hospital patients from opposite ends of the town who find themselves undergoing the same operation, they keep in touch to encourage one another.

MAY THE LORD MAKE YOU STRONG

He will strengthen you and keep you safe from the Evil One. Paul is a little anxious. Has he been too open and blunt? Perhaps he should have toned down his warnings about the deadly power of the Wicked One? Like children let into a horror film by mistake, will the young Christians who read his letter be trembling in their spiritual shoes? The balance must be put right. He therefore reminds them that they have a mighty ally in the Lord. In him they will find ample power and protection. They need never be defeated.

Quickly the spotlight passes from the Enemy to the Ally. 'The Lord' is mentioned seven more times between now and the end of the letter. Paul wants to leave us in no doubt. Christ has the leading role and occupies the centre of the stage.

And the Lord gives us confidence in you, and we are sure that you are doing and will continue to do what we tell you. If a soldier wants to win a battle he does not dive into a convenient bolt-hole and remain hidden. Instead, he remembers his training and advances according to plan. Paul is sure that his readers will not desert now that they are under fire. He would make a good general. He does not just drop hints. He gives commands.

Christ has the leading role and occupies the centre of the stage.

A skilful army officer knows how to get the best out of his troops. He asks a great deal from them, and they rise to his challenge. Paul does not simply rely on his gift to command. Nor does he put his faith in the calibre of his troops. He counts on the power and planning of his Commander-in-Chief, the Lord.

MAY THE LORD GIVE YOU STRENGTH TO ENDURE

Paul wants the Thessalonians to climb to their spiritual peak. For this they need to be open in a new way to God's love. They will then be able to return that love in active service.

Therefore he prays, **May the Lord lead you into a greater understanding of God's love and the endurance that is given by Christ.** They need to receive that sticking power which

134

Christ can give, even to the weakest. The Lord himself had a difficult mission to fulfil but he knew the power of God's Spirit all along the way. This helped him to face the demands others made on him. It gave him strength to put up with sneers. It even prepared him for the long lonely road which led to execution on the cross. He of all people can teach us how to love God and to keep going in his service.

This section has been all about prayer. It has taught us how important it is to pray. It has shown us how prayer forges links between people. If a man prays for you and asks you to pray for him, you are naturally drawn to him and he to you. So Paul's frank and warm-hearted touch helps to prepare the way for some straight talking to follow.

Work or starve

(3:6-15)

In Thessalonica a bee-hive situation had developed. In addition to the busy worker bees there were also layabout drones. Some of the Thessalonians had developed laziness to a fine art. And they did it from the best motives! They had expected heaven to come down any day now. So how could anyone expect them to dirty their hands with everyday work, when they were dressed in their Sunday best waiting for the Lord to appear?

In his first letter Paul had tried to deal with this problem. He had picked out the loafers and given them a straight talking to. There was no beating about the bush. 'Make it your aim to live a quiet life, to mind your own business, and to earn your own living, just as we told you before. In this way you will win the respect of those who are not believers, and you will not have to depend on anyone for what you need.' (1 Thessalonians 4:11, 12) And to make doubly sure that his message got across and some action was taken, he told the rest of the church to deal with layabouts firmly. They were to 'warn the idle' (1 Thessalonians 5:14) and not put up with laziness.

But in spite of Paul's lectures and letters on the subject, the idlers refused to take their hands out of their pockets. Not only were they becoming a burden on the Christian community, but they were also making themselves real nuisances. They had plenty of time on their hands and they knew how to use it. They began to meddle in other people's business. So yet again Paul takes up the cudgels. He gives some much-needed advice to the church on how to deal with Christian drones.

SEND THEM TO COVENTRY!

Our brothers, we command you in the name of our Lord Jesus Christ to keep away from all brothers who are living a lazy life and who do not follow the instructions that we gave them. Paul's teaching is very firm here. He gives a direct order, backed by the highest authority. Paul is an apostle, which means that Christ has given him authority to speak in his name. Therefore he expects the Thessalonians to fall into line. He will not listen to any 'ifs' or 'buts'.

The trade union movement was not the first to use the cold shoulder technique. It is a very effective way to deal with anyone who steps out of line. In Thessalonica the church was commanded to send its shirkers to Coventry. Such a course of action may seem a bit hard for a Christian fellowship, but we have to remember that these troublesome people were meddlers and busybodies. They had to be held at arm's length for the sake of everyone else.

136

However, hard-working church members must not over-react. Paul tells them to *keep away* from the lazy, not to *campaign against* them. In spite of their disobedience, the troublemakers are still Christian brothers and should be treated as such. The object of the exercise is not to drive them away, but to make them want to come running back. When a little child is naughty, sometimes the most effective punishment is simply to ignore him. After a while he will come running to his mother clamouring for attention.

The Bible makes it very clear that God is not just concerned about church services. He also cares about life and the daily grind. Our faith in Christ should affect our attitude to work. The deeply religious man need not be the one who sits cross-legged all day like an Eastern guru, lost in mystic thoughts. More often he is the man who is prepared to serve God in the course of earning his living. The Greeks were white-collar workers. They left the messy jobs to their slaves. In sharp contrast, the Jews were not afraid to roll up their sleeves and dirty their hands. They saw to it that every boy was taught a trade. No one was exempt. Even intellectuals like Paul had to have an ordinary job. He had studied hard and become a university teacher. He was a Member of Parliament too. Yet he had served an apprenticeship as a tentmaker. And at any time throughout his life he was prepared to take up the tools of his trade. You could see that Paul was not work-shy. You only had to look at his hands. They were as rough as any labourer's.

The Thessalonians had problems. When they became Christians, their decision made its mark on every corner of life. As a result, some were in danger of losing their jobs or being down-graded. After all, employers did not want people who adopted strange new religions. There was no telling what they might get up to.

Some of the Thessalonian converts were Greeks, not Jews. Because they were from another culture they had different ideas about work. They were proud of their office jobs and looked down on factory-floor workers. When they were expected to join them, they rebelled. They thought of manual labour as beneath their dignity, so if nothing else was available they stopped work altogether. They then became a burden on their Christian brothers who stayed at work and refused to join the dole queue. Although the idlers were too proud to work, they were evidently not too proud to sponge off others.

There was no excuse for this conduct. Paul had given clear instructions, backed by his personal example. **You yourselves know very well that you should do just what we did. We were not lazy when we were with you. We did not accept anyone's support without paying for it. Instead, we worked and toiled; we kept working day and night so as not to be an expense to any of you.** Paul's own working week would be a shop-steward's nightmare. It would take him back to the bad old days. Paul was anything but a nine-to-five, five-days-a-week man. Nor did he hold out for a tea-break and a full hour at lunch-time. He worked non-stop. He would do a full day's work and then go straight on to do a night-shift. And he made this superhuman effort for three reasons. Firstly, he needed to be an example. Secondly, he had to silence his critics. There were always some who thought of evangelism as a racket for making easy money. They would be the first to charge Paul with trying to get rich quick, if he passed the collection plate round too often. Thirdly, he did not want to be a financial drag on the young church. **We did this, not because we have no right to demand your support; we did it to be an example for you to follow.**

Elsewhere Paul gives some clear teaching on ministers' pay. Preachers of the gospel, he says, may live from what they earn by preaching. They need have no worries about that. There was nothing wrong in passing the collection plate round. (See, for example, 1 Corinthians 9:11-14) But

Paul's own pioneer job meant that he was constantly on the move. He had to go into situations which needed handling in different ways. Often he preferred to refuse offers of money for his personal support because he wanted to save himself from feeling in debt to any one group. This left him free to move on whenever he felt the right moment had come. God had given him a special roving commission, so he had to be very careful not to get bogged down with moral obligations to his financial supporters.

It recent years it has become popular with students to explore the world. They work their own passage and take jobs here and there. By this means they earn enough money for their keep and to pay for the next leg of the journey. Like them, Paul did not follow a fixed schedule. He soon found that his mission could not be fitted with a strait-jacket. He had to keep flexible and be prepared for sudden changes of plans as the Holy Spirit directed him.

REMEMBER OUR SLOGAN (vs. 10-12)

While we were with you we used to say to you, 'Whoever refuses to work is not allowed to eat.' We must be clear about the kind of people Paul has in mind when he writes this. He is not talking about those who cannot find a job. Nor is he including those too sick to go to work. He is speaking about healthy people who refuse point blank to dirty their hands. He is singling out those who are content to live off welfare. Wherever there are generous schemes providing sickness and unemployment benefits, there are always those who abuse the system. And the early churches were famous for their generosity. They were easy prey for spongers.

From the word go Paul had been afraid that this sort of thing might happen in Thessalonica. He had left them with a slogan, **Whoever refuses to work is not allowed to eat.** If that sounds like tough talk for a Christian leader, we have to be realistic. Some lazy people simply are not prepared to listen to a lecture. So Paul tried another way. If he could not reach the work-shy through their heads he would try their stomachs. If they went hungry for a while, the rumbles of their empty stomachs might speak more loudly than his words!

We say this because we hear that there are some people among you who live lazy lives and who do nothing except meddle in other people's business. These are the squad who have downed tools ready for the Lord's return from heaven. They are so heavenly minded that they are no earthly use. They want to have their cake and eat it. They are lazy, and yet busybodies. They do nothing to earn their own keep, but plenty to stop others earning theirs. Other people have a day's work to do, but these layabouts do nothing but get in their way. They criticize them and hold them up – the very people who supply their bread and butter! They are like the disgruntled hitch-hiker thumbing a lift from a passing motorist. When he has been picked up, he launches into a tirade against all car owners!

There are attractive features in the drop-out hippy culture. It makes an effective protest against the rat race when it underlines personal values. We have to wake up to the fact that our quality of life has little to do with the possession of material comforts. Yet the hippies represent over-reaction. They strum their guitars dreamily but do not provide an answer to any of today's pressing problems. Their lifestyle has a value as a symbol. It can never be a convincing alternative.

The layabouts in Thessalonica are in for a shock. They think they can sit around all day with their feet up. The boss will never find out. But they are mistaken. Paul keeps his ear to the ground. He likes to be well-informed about his Christian family, and there are plenty of friends who are travelling the region. They provide a fruitful 'grape-vine' of juicy information!

140

On hearing the news, Paul calls the slackers firmly to order. **In the name of the Lord Jesus Christ we command these people and warn them** ... There is no need to mention names. The culprits know who they are, the rest of the church knows – and they all know that Paul knows! He tells them **to lead orderly lives and work to earn their own living.** 'That's enough!' says Paul. 'Settle down to a routine. Don't drift. It's time you got a job, so start looking!'

KEEP ON THEIR TAILS (vs. 13-15)

Paul now turns to the rest of the church. They have a three-fold responsibility towards the lazy. First, to set an example. **But you, brothers, must not get tired of doing good.** Secondly, to make them ashamed. They will need sticking power when they try to deal with layabouts. Laziness cannot be cured in a day. Constant prods will be needed to win the work-shy back to an active life. And, even then, there is no guarantee of success. **It may be that someone there will not obey the message we send you in this letter. If so, take note of him and have nothing to do with him, so that he will be ashamed.**

And then, last but not least, the order of the day is LOVE. **But do not treat him as an enemy; instead, warn him as a brother.** So Paul comes to the end of his section on church discipline. He tells the church to balance sternness with gentleness. The object is not just to win the battle, but to win back the brother.

Goodbye and God bless

(3:16-18)

Some precious raw materials are only found in a limited number of places in the world. Countries which possess such rare assets are in a powerful bargaining position. They can fix the price and control the supply. Their customers know that they are at risk, and so spare no time, effort or money to find new deposits. The greater the number of sources of supply, the safer they feel.

In this closing section, Paul speaks of a very rare commodity, 'peace'. This has only one source, 'the Lord himself'. But there is no cause for anxiety, and no reason to search frantically elsewhere for substitutes. God's peace is free, the supply is generous, and the resources adequate for all who want it. So he can pray with real assurance, **May the Lord himself, who is our source of peace, give you peace at all times and in every way.**

Paul has spoken about problem people in both his letters. He is aware that there could be trouble when this second one is read to the congregation in Thessalonica. He has ticked off whole groups. Possibly they may be offended and go off in a huff. This would cause divisions in the church, so God's peace will be very much in demand. The cracks must not just be papered over, they must be cemented together.

Like a modern, all-purpose adhesive, God's peace is made to meet the needs of every situation. Paul cannot imagine any emergency in which it will not work. **May the Lord himself . . . give you peace at all times and in every way.** Divisions in the church can be caused by personality, age, race or background, but they need never be tolerated if God's peace is applied.

Peace is a favourite word of Paul's. We have already seen

142

that it means far more than simply an absence of strife. It has a positive ring. Peace means harmony and prosperity. It binds people from all sorts of backgrounds and outlooks into a single team. It is this that Paul has in mind when he adds, **The Lord be with you all.** We can only find true peace when the Prince of Peace is present.

At this point Paul takes the pen from his secretary and adds his personal greeting in his own distinctive handwriting. **With my own hand I write this: Greetings from Paul.** He does this for a very good reason. The church in Thessalonica needs to be certain that the letter is genuine. There will be some people who will try to brush it aside. 'Don't pay any attention to that,' they'll sneer. 'It's a fake!'

Already forged letters were beginning to appear in Paul's name, so now he makes it a rule always to add a few sentences in his own hand. **This is the way I sign every letter; this is how I write.** Today banks use the same safeguard. When a customer opens an account they ask him for a specimen signature. At any time his handwriting can then be compared with the signature on his cheques, and forgeries can be detected. So Paul tells his readers to take careful note. They are to keep this specimen of his handwriting for future reference.

Time and again during the course of these two letters, we have seen how God has provided for the Christians at Thessalonica. They have enjoyed a downpour of blessings, though they have not deserved a single drop. It is all due to Christ. He is the proof of God's generosity. So Paul's parting words give all his readers, past and present, heart for the future. The past supplies of God's undeserved love will never dry up. In this final blessing the scallywags are not separated from the saints. **May the grace of our Lord Jesus Christ be with you all.**

And so say all of us!